PRACTICAL ACCOUNTING FOR SMALL BUSINESSES

PRACTICAL ACCOUNTING FOR SMALL BUSINESSES

Second Edition

Laura Kirsner and Lyn Taetzsch

VNR VAN NOSTRAND REINHOLD COMPANY
NEW YORK CINCINNATI TORONTO LONDON MELBOURNE

Library of Congress Catalog Card Number: 82-23809
ISBN: 0-442-28420-9

Manufactured in the United States of America

Published by Van Nostrand Reinhold Company Inc.
135 West 50th Street, New York, N. Y. 10020

Van Nostrand Reinhold
480 Latrobe Street
Melbourne, Victoria 3000, Australia

Van Nostrand Reinhold Company Limited
Molly Millars Lane
Wokingham, Berkshire, England

15 14 13 12 11 10 9 8 7 6 5 4 3 2 1

Library of Congress Cataloging in Publication Data

Kirsner, Laura, 1945–
Practical accounting for small businesses.

Rev. ed. of: Practical accounting for small businesses/Lyn Taetzsch and Laura Taetzsch. 1978, c1977.
Bibliography: p.
Includes index.
1. Small business—Accounting. I. Taetzsch, Lyn. II. Taetzsch, Laura. Practical accounting for small businesses. III. Title.
HF5635.K64 1983 657′.9042 82-23809
ISBN 0-442-28420-9

To our husbands—Jim Kirsner and Adrian Epstein, and our children—Matthew, Stacey, Blixy, Owen, Eric, Daniel, and Marc.

Introduction

"What good is accounting? It's *making* money that's important—not keeping track of it. Making money is exciting, but recordkeeping is dull."

This is the typical attitude of today's entrepreneur. This is also why so many businesses fail every day.

No business can survive today without knowing if it *is* making a profit, and *how* it's making a profit. And that's what accounting is designed to do—to help you figure out whether or not you're making money, and how you're making it.

Suppose you manufacture two product lines, A and B. A is losing money, but B is making money. Without the proper accounting practices, you may never know this, and continue to dump money into the losing product.

The first function of accounting then is to keep track of the money you spend and the money you take in so that you know exactly what your investment is doing for you. Without this knowledge, you would have no idea whether to keep doing what you're doing, to change what you're doing, or to stop what you're doing.

FROM BOOKKEEPING TO MANAGERIAL ACCOUNTING

The basis for accounting is the double-entry bookkeeping system. This system is simply a method for recording all business income and expenditures in a methodical, logical manner. It's called "double-entry" because each amount is *entered,* or *written,* twice.

Why write everything down twice? Because the way the system was designed, this provides an accuracy check. Writing every item down twice also makes logical sense because there are two sides to every income or expenditure. If you spend cash to buy inventory, for example, this same amount should be recorded in two places: (1) *subtract from Cash,* and (2) *add to Inventory.*

You'll find more on the *theory* of double-entry bookkeeping in Chapter 1, and the *practical methods* for implementing it, in Chapter 3.

UNCLE SAM AND YOU

You may not have realized it, but one of your partners in business—whether you like it or not—is Uncle Sam. Many of the recordkeeping practices discussed in this book are necessary because you must comply with Internal Revenue Service regulations. Federal and state governments have a stake in your business in many ways. In addition to taking a cut of your profits, they want you to withhold and pay taxes on employees' salaries, and to collect and pay sales taxes.

You'll find methods for handling payroll and payroll taxes in Chapter 9, and sales taxes in Chapter 10.

As for the IRS, before you even *start* your business, you should consider the implications of the various legal forms your business might take—proprietorship, partnership or corporation. These issues are discussed in Chapter 2, "Starting Your Business."

CUSTOMIZING GENERAL ACCOUNTING PRACTICES TO YOUR PARTICULAR BUSINESS

While every business engages in the basic activities of taking money in and paying it out, (see Chapter 4 on "Cash," and Chapter 5 on "Purchases and Accounts Payable"), not every business sells on credit or keeps an inventory of goods. If you sell on credit, you'll find good advice in Chapter 7 on how to control credit and collections as well as how to handle the recordkeeping for this area. Chapter 6 covers the paperwork and recordkeeping for credit sales, including invoicing, credit memos and handling accounts receivable.

If you're in the retail business, you'll find special topics on "Retail Store Accounting" in Chapter 12. If you're in the manufacturing business, you'll need methods for "Accounting for Manufacturing Expenses" in Chapter 13.

MANAGERIAL ACCOUNTING

Chapter 14 is called "Managerial Accounting," but managerial accounting also includes Chapter 15 on "Cash Budgeting and Financial Planning" and Chapter 17 on "Internal Control."

Managerial accounting really starts with the preparation of two basic accounting reports: the income statement and the balance sheet (see Chapter 11). The *income statement* summarizes the business' activity over a period of time (one year, for example), while the *balance sheet* shows its assets and liabilities at a particular point in time (December 31, 1985, for example).

In Chapter 14 you'll find methods for analyzing the financial health of your business. You'll also learn how to make a break-even analysis, which can be helpful in deciding whether to take on a new line, whether an advertising campaign has been successful, or even to go into business in the first place.

In Chapter 15 you'll learn how to plan for your cash needs by making cash projections and budgets. And in Chapter 17 you'll see why internal controls are necessary, and how to prevent losses from theft or recordkeeping errors.

FORMS, SYSTEMS AND COMPUTERS

If your business is very small, you'll find the information you need on forms and systems in Chapter 18. But even small businesses today may want to explore the possibility of computerizing part of their accounting and other business functions. That's because there's been an enormous increase in the amount of computing power you can get today for the price.

Chapter 19 explores the ins and outs of computerizing your business. You'll find out when you should consider getting a computer and what types of functions would be best to computerize first. You'll also find a comparison of the various types of computers—microcomputer, minicomputer, and mainframe—and a discussion of purchasing, leasing or renting equipment. Finally, you'll find a checklist of things to look for when buying a computer.

To sum it all up—good accounting practices are as critical to your business' success as are solid sales and marketing practices. By recording what happens, and arranging those records in a meaningful form, accounting methods provide the means for smart management decision making—and that's what business success is all about.

Acknowledgments

We'd like to thank Tom Mitchell for the excellent chapter he wrote on computerized systems; Bruce Critchley for his help on the retail chapter; Ken Zweibel and Stan Stolar for their advice on income taxes; Bob Taetzsch for his review of the data processing information; Jim Kirsner for his work on the illustrations; and last, but certainly not least, Angela Harris for all the typing she did.

Contents

PRACTICAL ACCOUNTING FOR SMALL BUSINESSES

1

Accounting Theory

The purpose of accounting is to provide a systematic and logical method of keeping track of how a business is doing. The basic principles of accounting apply equally to a small business as well as a large one, although the implementation of these principles will naturally be more complex in a large corporation than in a small proprietorship.

In this chapter you'll get an overall view of basic accounting theory so you'll understand the principles behind the recordkeeping. In Chapter 3 we'll get into the practical implementation of this theory in a small business.

FINANCIAL STATEMENTS

Financial statements are the end products of information you'll be recording regularly about your business. The simple balance sheet and income statement (sometimes called a "profit and loss statement") in Figure 1.1 illustrates how accounting works. To begin our discussion of these statements, let's first define some terms.

Asset. Anything the company owns of monetary value (inventory, cash, equipment, real estate) plus money owed to the company.

Liability. Money the company owes others.

Owner's equity. A company's assets minus liabilities. Put another way, if all the company's assets of $70,000 were used to pay off all the company's liabilities of $40,000, there would be $30,000 of owners' equity left over.

Balance sheet. A statement showing the assets, liabilities, and owner's equity at a particular point in time.

Income statement. A statement showing a company's activity over a period of time, indicating the net profit or loss after cost of goods sold and operating expenses are subtracted from revenues (sales).

Cost of goods sold. In a retail operation, the wholesale price the company paid for the goods it sold; in a manufacturing operation, the total cost of raw materials plus labor and other costs involved in producing the items.

BALANCE SHEET AS OF 12/31/96

Assets		*Liabilities*	
Cash	$ 8,000	Accounts Payable	$ 5,000
Accounts Receivable	15,000	Loan Payable	33,000
Inventory	40,000	Sales Tax Payable	2,000
Equipment	7,000	*Total Liabilities*	40,000
		Owner's Equity	
		Owner's Capital	10,000
		Retained Earnings	20,000
Total Assets	$70,000	Liabilities + O.E.	$70,000

INCOME STATEMENT FROM 1/1/96 TO 12/31/96

Sales		$110,000
Cost of Goods Sold		80,000
Gross Profit		30,000
Operating Expenses		
Rent	3,000	
Utilities	500	
Salaries	10,500	
Advertising	2,000	
Insurance	500	
Sales Taxes	3,500	
Total Operating Expenses		20,000
Net Income		$ 10,000
Retained Earnings, Beginning of Year:		10,000
Retained Earnings, End of Year:		$ 20,000

FIGURE 1.1. Two simplified financial statements: A Balance Sheet and an Income Statement (sometimes called a "Profit and Loss Statement"). The Balance Sheet is for a particular point in time (12/31/96) and the Income Statement covers a period of time (1/1/96 to 12/31/96).

Gross profit. The profit after cost of goods sold is subtracted from sales, before other expenses of running the business are subtracted.

Operating expenses. Any costs incurred during the period in which the revenues were made, but not part of the cost of goods sold. (For example, rent, salaries, advertising, utilities.)

Net income. Profit left after subtracting operating expenses from gross profit.

Retained earnings. Profits that are retained in the company as working capital and not distributed to the owners of the company.

The business described in the financial statements in Figure 1.1 is a fictitious retail store that has been in business for two years at the time these statements were prepared. The balance sheet shows the financial status of the business at a particular point—the end of 1996. At that time the business had $8,000 in the bank. It had accounts receivable (money owed the business by its customers) of $15,000. By taking a physical inventory at the end of the year, the company found it had $40,000 worth of goods. And the various equipment it owned (store fixtures, cash registers, delivery truck, etc.) had a book value of $7,000 as of that date. This gave the business total assets of $70,000.

On the liability side, the business owed its suppliers $5,000 (accounts payable) and had a bank loan outstanding of $33,000. As of the date of the balance sheet it also owed $2,000 in sales taxes on merchandise it had already sold. This made the company's total liabilities $40,000.

By subtracting the liabilities from the assets, we see that the owner's equity in the business, or net worth, was $30,000 at that time. This $30,000 consisted of $10,000 in the owner's capital account (money the owner personally invested in the business) and $20,000 of retained earnings. Let's look at the income statement now and see where these retained earnings came from.

The income statement covers a *period* of time—in our example, the whole year beginning January 1, 1996, and ending December 31, 1996 (the date of the balance sheet). An income statement could cover a shorter period of time, such as a month or a quarter (3-month period). This statement shows *how* the company earned its income (or lost its losses).

The first figure listed on the income statement is "sales"—the revenues the company generated throughout the year by its sales efforts. Because this is a retail operation, we next subtract the cost of goods sold—the wholesale price paid for the goods that were sold. This leaves us a gross profit of $30,000.

There are, however, other costs involved in doing business throughout the year in order to make that $110,000 worth of sales. These costs are listed under operating expenses, and in this company's case they came to $20,000. By subtracting the $20,000 from the $30,000 gross profit, we get the net profit of $10,000. This is the amount of money the business made during that year.

The previous year the company also made profits of $10,000, and this is listed as "retained earnings, beginning of year." That $10,000 plus the

$10,000 made in 1996 were retained in the company (not paid out to owners) and the total $20,000 made during the two years gives the figure shown on the balance sheet as "retained earnings."

To sum it up, the balance sheet gives a complete financial picture of the company at one point in time. It shows what the business owns, what it owes, and the difference between these, which is owner's equity. An income statement shows the activity that took place during a period of time in order to earn the profits (or losses) which affect the amount of owner's equity on the balance sheet in the form of retained earnings.

THE ACCOUNTING EQUATION

You might have noticed from the example above that

$$\text{assets} = \text{liabilities} + \text{owner's equity}$$

This is called the "accounting equation." The left side of the equation must always equal the right side. If a business has assets of $100,000, for example, the liabilities plus owner's equity must also equal $100,000.

Let's look at a few simple examples to illustrate this point. Suppose you want to start a business, and you have $50,000 to invest in it. You open a bank acount in the business name and deposit the $50,000. Your business's balance sheet will now be as follows:

Assets		*Liabilities*	0
Cash	$50,000		
		Owner's Equity	
		Owner's Capital	$50,000
Total Assets	$50,000	Liabilities + O.E.	$50,000

Let's say you then buy $30,000 worth of inventory. You pay $20,000 cash and agree to pay the other $10,000 in 30 days (creating an accounts payable of $10,000). A look at the balance sheet now shows:

Assets		*Liabilities*	
Cash	$30,000	Accounts Payable	$10,000
Inventory	30,000		
		Owner's Equity	
		Owner's Capital	50,000
Total Assets	$60,000	Liabilities + O.E.	$60,000

Because you spent $20,000 of your cash, you have $30,000 left. There has been an increase in your assets, however, of $30,000 worth of inventory. This transaction has created an accounts payable of $10,000 which is listed as a liability.

Then suppose you take out a bank loan in order to buy $20,000 worth of equipment for your business. Your balance sheet now shows:

Assets		*Liabilities*	
Cash	$30,000	Accounts Payable	$10,000
Inventory	30,000	Loans Payable	20,000
Equipment	20,000		
		Owner's Equity	
		Owner's Capital	50,000
Total Assets	$80,000	Liabilities + O.E.	$80,000

Note that the $20,000 in equipment you bought is an asset on the balance sheet, and the $20,000 loan is a liability. As we can see from the above examples, no matter what activity your business engages in, the accounting equation always remains balanced:

assets = liabilities + owner's equity

RECORDING TRANSACTIONS

In the above examples, there were several business transactions: You used cash to buy inventory; you took out a loan; you bought equipment. Whenever your business is involved in receiving or paying out (goods, cash, or even a promise to pay), this is called a "transaction." Since so many transactions occur in the ordinary operations of a business, it would be tedious to draw up a new balance sheet for each. So accountants record these transactions on what are called "T-accounts." They are called this because they resemble a T. A T-account is set up for each asset, liability, or owner's equity account. The following are some examples:

CASH		INVENTORY		LOANS PAYABLE	
debit	credit	debit	credit	debit	credit

In case you're worried about those words "debit" and "credit," rest assured that they mean nothing more than "left" and "right." Debit is always the left side of the T-account and credit is always the right side of the T-account.

To show how transactions are recorded on T-accounts, let's start out with a new business in which the owner invests $100,000. When the $100,000 is deposited in the bank, the balance sheet appears as follows:

Assets		*Liabilities*	0
Cash	$100,000		
		Owner's Equity	
		Owner's Capital	$100,000
Total Assets	$100,000	Liabilities + O.E.	$100,000

This $100,000 investment is recorded on the following two T-accounts:

CASH	
debit	credit
100,000	

OWNER'S CAPITAL	
debit	credit
	100,000

Note that we increased the Cash account by debiting and the Owner's Capital account by crediting. The rules for increasing accounts are as follows:

Asset accounts are increased by debiting.
Liability accounts are increased by crediting.
Owner's Equity accounts are increased by crediting.

And the opposite it true:

Asset accounts are decreased by crediting.
Liability accounts are decreased by debiting.
Owner's Equity accounts are decreased by debiting.

Shown diagramatically,

Assets	=	Liabilities + Owner's Equity
plus (+) = debit (left)		plus (+) = credit (right)
minus (−) = credit (right)		minus (−) = debit (left)

In this way the accounting equation is kept in balance. Every transaction will always involve at least two T-accounts, and if the amount is entered as a debit on one account, it must be entered as a credit on the other.

There are various kinds of transactions. Some, for example, simply exchange one kind of asset for another. This would happen if $30,000 in cash were used to buy $30,000 worth of inventory. Cash would be decreased (credited) and Inventory would be increased (debited):

(asset account) CASH	
debit (+)	credit (−)
* 100,000	30,000

(asset account) INVENTORY	
debit (+)	credit (−)
30,000	

* Prior entry.

Note that the balance in the Cash account (debits minus credits) is now $70,000. Both Cash and Inventory are asset accounts, and therefore this transaction hasn't changed the total amounts of the left and right sides of the accounting equation on the balance sheet:

Assets		*Liabilities*	0
Cash	$ 70,000		
Inventory	30,000	*Owner's Equity*	
		Owner's Capital	$100,000
Total Assets	$100,000	Liabilities + O.E.	$100,000

In another type of transaction we increase both sides of the equation. Suppose $10,000 worth of supplies is purchased on credit, payable within 30 days. These supplies are an addition to the business's assets, but they also add a liability of an accounts payable:

(asset account) SUPPLIES	
debit (+)	credit (−)
10,000	

(liability account) ACCOUNTS PAYABLE	
debit (−)	credit (+)
	10,000

Looking at the balance sheet again, we now see:

Assets		*Liabilities*	
Cash	$ 70,000	Accounts Payable	$ 10,000
Inventory	30,000		
Supplies	10,000	*Owner's Equity*	
		Owner's Capital	100,000
Total Assets	$110,000	Liabilities + O.E.	$110,000

By adding $10,000 worth of supplies to the assets and $10,000 worth of accounts payable to the liabilities, we increased both sides of the equation by $10,000.

In another type of transaction we simply exchange one liability for another, which leaves the total of both sides of the equation the same. Suppose the owner gives a $5,000 interest bearing note to his supplier so that he doesn't have to pay the full $10,000 account payable within the 30 day period. This is how the T-account would look:

(liability account)
ACCOUNTS PAYABLE

debit (−)	credit (+)
5,000	* 10,000

(liability account)
NOTES PAYABLE

debit (−)	credit (+)
	5,000

* Prior entry.

Note that the balance in Accounts Payable (credits minus debits) is now $5,000. Let's see how this transaction looks on the balance sheet:

Assets		*Liabilities*	
Cash	$ 70,000	Accounts Payable	$ 5,000
Inventory	30,000	Notes Payable	5,000
Supplies	10,000		
		Owner's Equity	
		Owner's Capital	100,000
Total Assets	$110,000	Liabilities + O.E.	$110,000

In another type of transaction we *decrease* both sides of the equation. Suppose $5,000 cash is used to pay off the $5,000 of accounts payable. This is recorded on T-accounts as follows:

(asset account)
CASH

debit (+)	credit (−)
† 100,000	† 30,000
	5,000

(liability account)
ACCOUNTS PAYABLE

debit (−)	credit (+)
† 5,000	† 10,000
5,000	

† Prior entries.

Note that the Cash balance (debits minus credits) is now $65,000 and the Accounts Payable balance (credits minus debits) is now zero. The following shows how the transaction affects the balance sheet:

Assets		*Liabilities*	
Cash	$ 65,000	Notes Payable	5,000
Inventory	30,000		
Supplies	10,000	*Owner's Equity*	
		Owner's Capital	100,000
Total Assets	$105,000	Liabilities + O.E.	$105,000

Note that the assets have been decreased by $5,000 cash and the liabilities have been decreased by $5,000 accounts payable.

RECORDING REVENUES AND EXPENSES

Note that none of the above transactions affected owner's equity. The only way to affect owner's equity is to generate sales, incur expenses, or add or withdraw capital. When revenues (sales) are generated, both the income statement and the balance sheet are affected. Let's assume the above company makes a credit sale (on account) of $10,000. The cost of goods sold is $7,000, leaving a profit of $3,000 (we won't worry about operating costs in this example). In order to record this transaction, four (rather than two) T-accounts are used:

(asset account)
ACCOUNTS RECEIVABLE

debit (+)	credit (−)
10,000	

(income statement account)
SALES

debit (−)	credit (+)
	10,000

(asset account)
INVENTORY

debit (+)	credit (−)
* 30,000	7,000

(income statement account)
COST OF GOODS SOLD

debit (+)	credit (−)
7,000	

* Prior entry.

Note that Revenues or Sales accounts are increased by crediting. All income accounts are increased by crediting. All expense accounts, such as Rent, Salaries, Utilities, Advertising, and Insurance Expense are increased by debiting. In all double-entry recordkeeping, of course, a figure entered on the left side of one account must be entered on the right side of another account.

The $10,000 sale on account is entered on the left (debit) side of Accounts Receivable (an asset because it is money owed the business) and the right (credit) side of Sales. We used up $7,000 worth of inventory, however, to make this sale, decreasing the Inventory account by entering this amount on the right (credit) side. The same $7,000 is listed on the left (debit) side of Cost of Goods Sold.

Let's look at the balance sheet and income statement immediately after this transaction:

BALANCE SHEET

Assets		*Liabilities*	
Cash	$ 65,000	Notes Payable	$ 5,000
Inventory	23,000		
Supplies	10,000	*Owner's Equity*	
Accounts		Owner's Capital	100,000
Receivable	10,000	Retained Earnings	3,000
		Total O.E.	103,000
Total Assets	$108,000	Liabilities + O.E.	$108,000

INCOME STATEMENT

Sales	$10,000
Cost of Goods Sold	7,000
Income	$ 3,000
Retained Earnings: $3,000	

Note first the changes on the balance sheet. Inventory was reduced from $30,000 to $23,000 because $7,000 of it was used in the $10,000 sale. Accounts Receivable of $10,000 were added to the balance sheet as an asset. This decrease of $7,000 and increase of $10,000 made a net increase on the asset side of $3,000, bringing the total from the previous $105,000 to $108,000.

On the right side of the balance sheet, $3,000 in retained earnings was added to the owner's equity, bringing the total of owner's equity and liabilities from $105,000 to $108,000. The $3,000 in retained earnings is the profit from the $10,000 sale, as shown on the income statement. Sales minus cost of goods sold equals the $3,000 profit.

In this chapter accounting theory has been presented in a nutshell. The rest of the book is simply an expansion of the above principles. If you have found it difficult to grasp the theory in one gulp, however, you should go on to the next chapters, in which more detailed illustrations of the use of this theory will be given. You can then come back and reread this chapter, and you'll find that it makes more sense as you see the practical applications.

2

Starting Your Business Initial Tax Planning and Other Considerations

Before you start your business, there are several decisions you must make which can have a major impact on the amount of income taxes you'll pay in the future. Following is a brief discussion of the points you should discuss with a tax expert.

ACTIVITY FOR A PROFIT

You know that you are entering into your business to make a profit, but this may not convince the Internal Revenue Service that your business isn't just a hobby.

Many small businesses begin as sidelines—the owner continues to work at another job until his business gets off the ground. This could create a special tax problem when your business loses money. If you have continued losses for several years, the IRS may question the deductibility of these losses on your tax return, and say that your business is really a hobby, carried on for your personal satisfaction and not for profits. This is especially true if your business involves recreation, such as running a charter boat or breeding horses.

If you expect to lose money on your sideline business, be prepared to convince the IRS of your profit-making intentions. If you can show that your business is in a field in which you are an expert, that losses are a result of unusual circumstances or start-up costs, or that you have a reasonable expectation of making a profit, your losses will be deductible.

The IRS will generally presume that you're engaged in a business activity if you produce a profit in any two out of five consecutive years (seven consecutive years if the activity is primarily the breeding, training, showing, or racing of horses.). If you don't make a profit for two years in the five-year period, or if the two years of profit don't convince the IRS that you're in business for a profit, you'll have to support your position with other evidence about the nature of your business.

CHOOSING THE FORM OF YOUR BUSINESS

Once you've decided to start a business, you must decide what type of business entity to use. You can use the form of a *sole proprietorship,* a *partnership,* or a *corporation.* Which form is best for you will depend on legal, tax, and practical considerations.

Sole Proprietorship

A sole proprietorship is the simplest form of business organization. You can form a sole proprietorship without filling out a single form. Not until you open a checking account, register your trademark, or hire employees will the paperwork begin. You can terminate the business without formalities, too.

A sole proprietorship can have only one owner. From a legal and tax perspective, it has no existence apart from its owner. The business' assets are your assets, and its liabilities are your liabilities. The amount of the income or loss of your business is entered as an item of income or loss on your individual income tax return (summarized on Schedule C). You must include your business income with your personal income whether or not you've taken the income out of the business.

The fact that the income and losses of a sole proprietorship are included in the owner's tax return will generally be advantageous. Obviously it will be nice to deduct your business losses from your other non-business income. Unless you're in a high income tax bracket you may be better off including the business income with personal income rather than being taxed as a corporation.

If you are a sole proprietor you can report your income on the accrual basis even though your non-business income is on the cash basis. Your tax year end for non-business income must be the same as your business year end.

If a significant amount of your income is from your business, you must file a quarterly declaration of estimated tax and make estimated tax payments to avoid paying a penalty to the IRS. This is to replace the withholding taxes you would pay if you were employed. You must also pay a self-employment tax for social security coverage.

Unlimited liability is one of the prime disadvantages of a sole proprietorship. You are personally liable for all debts your business incurs. Therefore, the amount of money you can lose isn't limited by the amount you invest. If a customer or employee should sue for personal injury, you will be personally liable. One reason that many business owners incorporate is to limit this liability.

Another disadvantage of a sole proprietorship is that death of the proprietor automatically terminates the business. If you want to assure the continuation of your business for your heirs, be sure you discuss this with your lawyer and prepare a will.

Partnership

A partnership is the relationship existing between two or more persons who join together to carry on a trade or business. Although a partnership can exist without a written agreement, we recommend that a formal agreement be prepared. This agreement should spell out how much money, property, labor, etc. each partner is to contribute, and how partnership income and losses are to be distributed.

A partnership, like a sole proprietorship, is not a taxable entity. Gains and losses must be included in the partners' individual tax returns. Nevertheless, a partnership must file an informational tax return, indicating how much income will be reported by each partner.

One of the disadvantages of a partnership is that no partner can report a loss in excess of his or her *basis,* or the amount he or she has invested in the business. This is not true for a sole proprietorship.

Like a proprietorship, each owner of a partnership has unlimited liability. The amount of money a partner can lose is not limited to the amount of money invested in the business. If the partnership is sued, each partner is liable for damages.

For a detailed description of how to account for a partnership, see Chapter 16.

Corporation

A corporation is a legal entity separate from its owners and employees. It's not as easy to start as a sole proprietorship. Unless you're well versed in business law you'll probably need a lawyer to set up your corporation.

Some advantages of the corporate form of business are:

- *Limited liability.* Since a corporation is a separate legal entity, its owners generally can't lose more than their investment. Officers of a corporation, however, may be legally responsible for any illegal acts of the corporation.

- *Ability to raise capital.* Capital can be raised by issuing stock in the corporation. Thus, a corporation can have many more owners, and therefore more sources of capital, than any other form of business.
- *Tax advantages.* Discussed in detail below.

When you set up a corporation, you have a choice of paying taxes on corporate income in one of two ways:

- Subchapter S Corporation.
- Ordinary corporation.

Subchapter S Corporation. If you elect to be taxed as a subchapter S corporation, you can operate your business as a corporation, but the corporation doesn't pay taxes as a separate entity.

The corporation must file an informational return with the Internal Revenue Service and shareholders report their proportional shares of the corporation's income or loss on their individual tax returns.

A subchapter S corporation will benefit you in the start-up stage of your business when you're losing money. You'll be able to deduct the losses from your ordinary income on your tax return. Like a partnership, the amount of loss you can deduct can't exceed the amount of money you have invested in the business, including loans. The subchapter S election can be terminated when the business becomes profitable.

To qualify as a subchapter S corporation, you must meet certain Internal Revenue Service tests regarding matters such as who can own stock, and the sources of the corporation's income. You should consult a tax specialist before making this choice.

Subchapter S is useful for individuals who want the limited liability of a corporation but wish to be treated like a partnership or sole proprietorship for income tax purposes.

Ordinary Corporation. A corporation is a taxable entity. Any income not withdrawn as salary, interest, or other tax deductible expense is subject to tax. Any amounts withdrawn by the corporation's owners in the form of salary and interest on loans are deducted from the corporation's income before taxes are computed. Any further withdrawals of corporate funds will be in the form of dividends. Dividends are not tax deductible expenses for the corporation, but the receiver of the dividend must pay personal income taxes on them. This is what is generally known as "double taxation" on corporate earnings. The subchapter S corporation avoids this double tax.

There are two possible ways for an ordinary corporation to avoid this double taxation. One way is to pay yourself and other shareholders *all* the corporation's earnings in the form of salary, which is a tax deductible expense to the corporation. You must be careful, however, that salary levels are "reasonable", or the IRS may consider high salary payments as dividends. Your accountant will be able to help you determine reasonable salaries for the owners of your business.

The other method of avoiding double taxation is to accumulate the earnings of the corporation; that is, not withdraw earnings in the form of high salaries or dividends until you liquidate the corporation. At that time you'll pay a capital gains tax, the rate of which should be lower than your individual tax rate. But beware that the IRS may limit the amount of earnings you can accumulate. At this writing, any amount over $250,000 ($150,000 if the principal function of the business is service) must be justified as necessary to run the business.

CHOOSING AN ACCOUNTING PERIOD

You may report your business income for tax purposes either on a calendar year (January 1–December 31) or on a fiscal year (any 12-month period). You should choose your business year end based on the nature of your business and the possible tax consequences.

Many retail store owners use January 31 as the end of their fiscal year since it coincides with the end of the Christmas and winter season. Inventory is generally at its lowest level at that time and more easily counted.

If your business is a sole proprietorship, your business year end must be the same as your personal year end, generally December 31. A partnership generally can't adopt a tax year other than that of all the principal partners unless approved by the IRS.

It's a good idea to consult a tax specialist when choosing your business' tax year end. Since you'll need IRS permission to change your year end, you must select it carefully.

CHOOSING YOUR ACCOUNTING METHOD

There are two basic accounting methods, or rules, which determine when you record income and expenses for your business: *the cash and accrual methods.* The Internal Revenue Service requires that you choose one of these methods and use it consistently from year to year. If the production, purchase, or sale of inventories is an income-producing factor of your business (such as in retail or manufacturing), you will have to use the accrual method for tax purposes. A service business might find that the cash basis is easiest to use and that it clearly reflects income.

Cash Method. If you use the cash method, you'll record income in the tax year you actually or "constructively" receive it. Suppose, for example, you have a December 31 year end and bill a customer for services rendered in December, 1985. If the customer pays you in January 1986, you'll report the income in 1986 even though the service was rendered in 1985.

"Constructively" received means that the funds are subject to your control, even if you may not have received them. Interest earned on a savings account is constructively received in the year it's earned, not when you actually take it out of the bank.

Under the cash method, expenses are deducted from income in the year you actually pay them, not when they are incurred or come due. Using the cash method thus allows you to control your taxable income to some extent. You can pay expenses early or postpone paying them in order to get the deduction in the year it will benefit you the most. Unfortunately, you may not use the cash method if you have inventories.

Accrual Method. Under this method, all income items are included in taxable income in the year you earn them, even though you receive payment in another tax year. Suppose, for example, you have a taxable year end of December 31 and bill a customer in December, 1987. Even if the customer doesn't pay this bill until 1988, you count it as income in 1987.

Likewise, expenses are deducted from income in the year you incur them, whether or not you pay for them in the same year.

SUMMING UP

Before you start your business, you should consider what form of business will be best for you: sole proprietorship, partnership or corporation. There are legal, tax, and practical advantages and disadvantages to each form. Your accountant and lawyer are the best people to help you make this choice. Then your accountant can help you with other tax planning matters—your accounting period and accounting method. A little "up-front" planning may save you money and prevent future aggravation.

3

Setting Up And Using Journals And Ledgers

In Chapter 1 you saw how the financial transactions of a business are recorded in T-accounts. The type and number of accounts used will depend on the nature of the business and whether it is on the cash or accrual basis of accounting for tax purposes (discussed in Chapter 2).

Remember that keeping records on a cash basis means you record income and expenses at the time you receive or pay out cash. When you pay the rent or write a payroll check, you record rent or salary expense.

If you keep records on an accrual basis, you record income when earned, and expenses when incurred, even if you do not actually receive or make payment. For example, if you bill a customer for $100 in July and receive payment in August, the $100 is considered part of July sales (on the cash basis it would be considered part of August sales). Similarly, expenses are recorded when incurred, whether or not they are paid at that time. For example, if you receive $500 worth of supplies in March which you pay for in April, the $500 is charged as an expense in March, not April.

You may want to use a combination of methods that will suit your particular needs. Since the cash basis is simpler, some companies keep their daily records with this method, making adjustments at the end of the year to reflect the accrual method. In the chapters that follow, systems for cash and accrual will be presented, depending on the particular situation.

A LIST OF T-ACCOUNTS

The following T-accounts are some typical ones used by many businesses. Receivables and Payables accounts refer to the accrual method of accounting. Receivables is money owed your company and Payables is money you owe others. This list does not include special accounts for retail and manufacturing companies such as Inventory and Cost of Goods Sold. (See individual chapters for specific information.) The accounts you use will depend on the kind of business you have. You should establish an account for each kind of asset, liability, revenue and expense your business has.

Asset Accounts. Asset accounts are increased by debiting, decreased by crediting.

Cash. Includes all cash held by the business in bank accounts, petty cash, cash registers, etc.

Accounts receivable. Sales that have been invoiced (for goods shipped or services rendered) but not yet paid for.

Notes receivable. Money owed the company in the form of notes or promises to pay.

Property. Buildings, land, or other real estate owned and used by the business.

Equipment. Machinery and other equipment owned by the business.

Vehicles. Trucks, cars, and other vehicles owned by the business.

Liability Accounts. Liability accounts are increased by crediting, decreased by debiting.

Accounts payable. Money the company owes others for good or services already received.

Notes payable. Outstanding notes and loans the company owes.

Sales taxes payable. Sales taxes the company owes on goods already sold.

Payroll taxes payable. Payroll taxes the company has not yet paid but owes for work already performed. (For example, if a company is required to deposit payroll taxes every three months, at the end of one month the Payroll Taxes Payable account will include taxes owed on the salaries paid out that month.)

Owner's Equity Accounts. Owner's equity accounts keep track of the capital invested and withdrawn from the company by owners, plus the earnings retained by the company. These accounts are increased by crediting and decreased by debiting.

Owner's capital account. The balance of the capital an owner has invested in the business. (In a partnership, there will be an owner's capital account for each partner.)

Retained earnings. Any earnings the company retains (not distributed to owners, stockholders, etc.)

Income Statement Accounts: Revenues. Sales of products, merchandise and services, and other earnings such as interest and rents. Revenue accounts, also referred to as income accounts, are increased by crediting and decreased by debiting.

Income Statement Accounts: Expenses. The costs of running a business. Expense accounts are increased by debiting and decreased by crediting.

Salaries expense. Money paid or owed to employees for services.

Payroll tax expense. Payroll taxes paid or owed.

Rent expense. Rent on the building in which a company is doing business.

Utilities expense. Cost of heat, lighting, phone, etc.

Insurance expense. Liability, auto, and other insurance costs of the business.

Interest expense. Interest on notes and loans.

Supplies expense. Cost of supplies used by the business.

Miscellaneous expense. Items that do not fall under other headings.

GENERAL LEDGER

The group of T-accounts that you set up for your business's recordkeeping is called the "General Ledger." There are various systems available (see Chapter 18) for keeping a general ledger of accounts. Figure 3.1 illustrates a

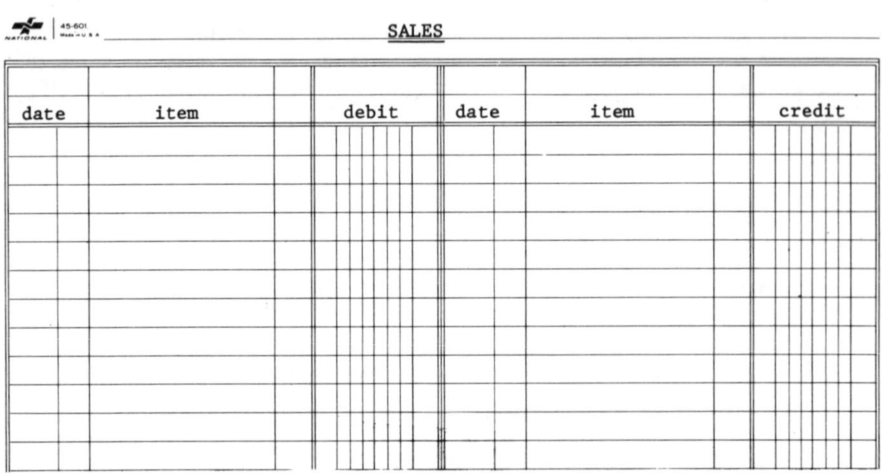
SALES

date	item	debit	date	item	credit

FIGURE 3.1. A "Sales" T-account. Debit items are recorded on the left side and credit items on the right.

T-account set up on lined columnar pad paper. Note that there are columns for listing the date and description as well as the amount of each debit or credit.

Entering all a business's daily financial transactions in the General Ledger as they occur poses several problems. First, it would be tedious to search through the General Ledger for the appropriate accounts each time you had a transaction to record. Second, you might forget to record each transaction properly as a debit on one account and a credit on its corresponding account. Third, you would have no chronological record of the business's activities easily observable in one place. For these reasons you'll want to keep a Cash Disbursements Journal (where all outgoing cash is recorded), a Cash Receipts Journal (where all incoming money is recorded), and a General Journal (to record all other transactions). You may also want to keep a Sales Journal if you bill your customers (see Chapter 6). These journals are kept on a day-to-day basis as transactions occur. Then once a month the information is posted in total to the General Ledger (T-accounts).

CASH DISBURSEMENTS JOURNAL

Whenever you write a check on your business bank account, you'll list it in the Cash Disbursements Journal. Figure 3.2 is an example of how a page in a typical Cash Disbursements Journal should be set up. Note that there's a place to record the date, the payee, the check number, and the total amount. Then on the right you'll want a column for each major disbursement area, such as Rent, Salaries, Payroll Taxes, and Utilities. Columns called "General" and "General Account Name" will be used to list items that don't have a separate column heading.

Every day as you write checks you'll record each item in the Cash Disbursements Journal. Check numbers should be listed in order, including voided checks, to be sure none are omitted. The "Payee" will be the name of the person, or company, to whom the check is made out. The total amount of the check should be listed under "total" and then again in the proper account column. If you have no column set up for an item, put it in the "General" column. (See Figure 3.3, which illustrates the recording of several typical transactions.)

At the end of the month you'll total the columns in the Cash Disbursements Journal as shown in Figure 3.4. Note that the sum of the Rent, Salaries, Payroll Taxes, Utilities, and General columns equal the sum of the "total" column. You are now ready to post these totals in your General Ledger. The total amount of the cash disbursements for the month should be listed as a credit in the Cash account. List the rent total as a debit in the Rent

CASH DISBURSEMENTS JOURNAL Page______

WILSON JONES G 7112

	date	payee	1 check #	2 total	3 Rent	4 Salaries	5 Payroll Taxes	6 Utilities	7 General	8 Gen. Acct. Name
1										
2										
3										
4										
5										
6										
7										
8										
9										
10										
11										
12										
13										
14										
15										
16										
17										
18										
19										
20										

FIGURE 3.2. Page from a Cash Disbursements Journal with separate columns for rent, salaries, payroll taxes, and utilities. Set up Cash Disbursements Journal to fit individual needs. If you want to separate your business' expenses into more expense categories than shown here, use accounting paper with more columns.

CASH DISBURSEMENTS JOURNAL Page 1

	date	payee	check# (1)	total (2)	Rent (3)	Salary (4)	Payroll tax (5)	Utility (6)	General Amount (7)	General Account (8)	9	10
1	4 1	J. Markum	2034	450 –	450 –							
2	4 2	United Bank	2035	143 25			143 25					
3	4 4	Office Supply Co.	2036	14 95					14 95	office supply		
4		VOID	2037									
5	4 6	Bell Tell.	2038	61 80				61 80				
6												
7												
8												
9												
10												
11												
12												
13												
14												
15												
16												
17												
18												
19												
20												
21												
22												
23												
24												
25												

FIGURE 3.3. Page from a Cash Disbursements Journal showing several entries. Note that the office supplies payment of $14.95 is listed under "general."

CASH DISBURSEMENTS JOURNAL Page____

date	payee	check #	total	Rent	Salary	Payroll tax	Utilities	General Amount	General Account
4-17	J.C. Power Co.	2078	59.35				59.35		
4-20	Local Gas	2079	10.95					10.95	Fuel Ex.
4-26	L. Benson	2080	242.30		242.30				
	R. Smith	2081	238.76		238.76				
4-30	General Tool Co.	2082	97.30					97.30	Tools Ex.
			2084.11 ✓	450.– ✓	973.40 ✓	143.25 ✓	166.45 ✓	351.01	

FIGURE 3.4. Page from a Cash Disbursements Journal showing monthly totals. Note the check marks next to the monthly amounts in the total, rent, salaries, payroll taxes, and utilities columns. These check marks mean the amounts have been posted to the General Ledger accounts.

account, salaries as a debit in the Salaries account, and so forth. Each time you make an entry, put a red check mark next to the amount in the Cash Disbursements Journal so you'll know it has been posted.

Each item in the general column will have to be posted individually to the proper account and each amount checked off as you post it to avoid duplicate posting (see Figure 3.5).

Looking at the Salaries T-account shown in Figure 3.6, you'll see that a column called "folio" has been added. When posting an item from the Cash Disbursements Journal into the General Ledger, you should make a note under "folio" which indicates where you got the information. In the example shown, the amount was taken from CD-2, the second page of the Cash Disbursements Journal. If you post an item from other journals, such as the Cash Receipts Journal, you would list this information under "folio" in a similar manner. This way you can always check back to see where information was obtained.

Figure 3.7 shows a sample Cash Disbursements monthly summary. These totals are posted to General Ledger accounts in Figure 3.8. "CD-3" is marked in the folio column of each ledger entry to indicate that the information was taken from the third page of the Cash Disbursements Journal. Note that the total cash disbursements are credited to Cash and debited to each of the expense accounts involved.

CASH RECEIPTS JOURNAL

The Cash Receipts Journal is a listing of all the money deposited into your business bank account. Cash receipts might include: cash, checks, and credit card payments received from customers on cash (as opposed to "on account") sales; payments of open accounts by customers; money invested in the business by its owners; refunds from suppliers; and rents received from tenants.

Figure 3.9 illustrates a page in a Cash Receipts Journal. How you will set up your Cash Receipts Journal will depend on what sources of income your business has, and how much information you need for your records.

Following is an explanation of the use of the various columns in the illustration:

Item. Use this for the source of the cash, check, etc. If you do not need a record of your payor, such as if you sell for cash, you might only total the day's receipts and list as "daily receipts" as shown in line 2 of this illustration.

Cash Disbursements Journal Page 2

	date	payee	check #	total	Rent	Salaries	Payroll tax	Utilities	General Amount	General Account
1	4-17	J.C. Power Co.	2078	59.35				59.35		
2	4-20	Local Gas	2079	10.95					10.95 ✓	Fuel ex.
3	4-26	L. Benson	2080	242.30		242.30				
4		R. Smith	2081	238.76		238.76				
5	4-30	General Tool Co.	2082	97.30					97.30 ✓	Tools Ex.
6				2084.11 ✓	450.– ✓	973.40 ✓	143.25 ✓	166.45 ✓	351.01	

FIGURE 3.5. This is the same Cash Disbursements Journal page as Figure 3.4. Note that the two items listed in the general column have been checked off to indicate they have been posted to the General Ledger accounts.

SALARIES EXPENSE

date	items	folio	debits	date	items	folio	credits
4-30		CD-2	973.40				

FIGURE 3.6. Salaries Expense account with "CD-2" written under the "folio" column to indicate that the April payroll amount of $973.40 was taken from page 2 of the Cash Disbursements Journal.

CASH DISBURSEMENTS JOURNAL Page 3

date	payee	check #	total	Salaries	Supplies	General Amount	General Account
4-3	Bell Tel.	3029	62.30			62.30 ✓	Tel. Ex.
	Void	3030					
4-15	L. Markowitz	3031	425-	425-			
	J. Mendem	3032	389-	389-			
	S. Johnson	3033	398-	398-			
4-20	Ace Co.	3034	215-		215-		
4-23	OK Ins. Co.	3035	52-			52- ✓	Ins. Ex.
4-25	Ellery Co.	3036	150-		150-		
4-30	Lease-A-Bldg. Co.	3037	600-			600- ✓	Rent Ex.
	L. Markowitz	3038	425-	425-			
	J. Mendem	3039	389-	389-			
	S. Johnson	3040	398-	398-			
			3503.30 ✓	2424- ✓	365- ✓	714.30	

FIGURE 3.7. Monthly totals on this Cash Disbursements Journal have been posted to the General Ledger accounts illustrated in Figure 3.8.

CASH

date	items	folio	debits	date	items	folio	credits
				4 30		CD-3	3503.30

FIGURE 3.8. Entries in these General Ledger accounts were taken from page 3 of the Cash Disbursements Journal shown in Figure 3.7.

SALARIES EXPENSE

NATIONAL 17-459 18-459 LEDGER WHITE EYE-EASE

date	items	folio	debits	date	items	folio	credits
4-30		CD-3	2424 -				

FIGURE 3.8. (Continued.)

SUPPLIES EXPENSE

NATIONAL 17-459 WHITE 18-459 EYE-EASE LEDGER

date	items	folio	debits	date	items	folio	credits
4-30		CD-3	365 –				

FIGURE 3.8. (Continued.)

TELEPHONE EXPENSE

date	items	folio	debits	date	items	folio	credits
4-30		CD-3	62.30				

FIGURE 3.8. (Continued.)

INSURANCE EXPENSE

date	items	folio	debits	date	items	folio	credits
4-30		CD-3	52-				

NATIONAL 17-459 WHITE 18-459 EYE-EASE LEDGER

FIGURE 3.8. (Continued.)

RENT EXPENSE

date	items	folio	debits	date	items	folio	credits
4-30		CD-3	600 -				

FIGURE 3.8. (Continued.)

CASH RECEIPTS JOURNAL Page CR-12

			1	2	3	4	5	6	
				total	Cash	Accounts	General		
	date	item	amount	deposit	Sales	Receivable	account	amount	
1		Balance from CR-11	12459 50		5010 -	7449 50			1
2	5-28	Daily Receipts	201 -		201 -				2
3	5-28	Martha Eagen	25 -				empl. loans	25 ✓	3
4	5-28	Herb's Luncheonette	247 50			247 50			4
5	5-28	Arrow Shops	43 -	516 50		43 -			5
6	5-29	Arco Products	97 -			97 -			6
7	5-29	ABC Co.	97 -			97 -			7
8	5-29	Thompson Co.	109 -			109 -			8
9	5-29	Daily Receipts	470 -	773 -	470 -				9
10	5-31	Lyn Taetzsch	500 -				owner's acct.	500 - ✓	10
11	5-31	Daily Receipts	347 50		347 50				11
12	5-31	Masko Co.	20 -	867 50			supplies ex.	20 - ✓	12
13			14616 50 ✓		6028 50 ✓	8043 - ✓		545 -	13
14									14
15									15
16									16
17									17
18									18
19									19
20									20
21									21
22									22
23									23
24									24
25									25

FIGURE 3.9. Page from Cash Receipts Journal showing monthly totals that are posted to the General Ledger accounts illustrated in Figure 3.10. Note the check marks indicating items have been posted.

Amount. This column is for the amount of the check, total daily receipts, etc.

Total deposit. This is the sum of all the amounts listed in the "amount" column which are included in one bank deposit. The purpose of this column is to match the amounts with the deposits on the bank statement when you reconcile your cash account (see Chapter 4). The total of this column should agree with the total of the "amount" column.

Cash Sales. The term "cash sale" means a sale which is paid for at the time of sale; that is, not billed. Payment may be in the form of cash, checks or bank credit card.

Accounts Receivable. List here all monies received in payment of invoices previously billed to customers and recorded in the Sales Journal (see Chapter 6).

General. These two columns are to record monies received from any sources for which you have no separate column. The general ledger account to which the item will be posted goes in column 5 and the amount goes in column 6.

At the end of each month you'll total the columns in the Cash Receipts Journal and post the totals to the General Ledger (see Figures 3.9 and 3.10). The total of the "amount" column is debited to Cash. The amounts in the other columns are credited to the various accounts. Note that the total of the "amount" column must be equal to the sum of all the other columns combined (not including the "deposit" column). Thus, you'll be entering the same amount of debits as credits to the General Ledger. If they aren't equal, your books will be out of balance. The "deposit" column is only used for bank reconciliation purposes; it's not posted to the General Ledger.

Note that the amounts in the "general" column are posted individually to the General Ledger in Figure 3.10. The $25.00 credit to the Employee Loan account is a reduction of an asset, a loan receivable.

The $500.00 credit to the Owner's Account represents money the owner invested in the business, an increase in an equity account. The $20.00 credited to Supplies Expense represents a refund from a supplier. This will reduce the expense.

GENERAL JOURNAL

The General Journal is used to record transactions which aren't entered in the Cash Receipts, Cash Disbursements or other journals. It may also be used to make an adjustment to your records for an error made in one of the

CASH

date	items	folio	debits	date	items	folio	credits
5-31		CR-11	14616 50				

FIGURE 3.10. Entries posted in these General Ledger accounts taken from the Cash Receipts Journal illustrated in Figure 3.9.

SALES

NATIONAL 17-459 WHITE 18-459 EYE-EASE LEDGER	date	items	folio	debits	date	items	folio	credits
					5-31		CR-12	6028 50

FIGURE 3.10. (Continued.)

ACCOUNTS RECEIVABLE

17-459 WHITE
18-459 EYE-EASE
LEDGER

date	items	folio	debits	date	items	folio	credits
				5-31		CR-12	8043 -

FIGURE 3.10. (Continued.)

EMPLOYEE LOANS

17-459 18-459 NATIONAL LEDGER WHITE EYE-EASE	date	items	folio	debits	date	items	folio	credits
					5-31		CR-12	25-

FIGURE 3.10. (Continued.)

NATIONAL 17-459 18-459 WHITE EYE EASE LEDGER

OWNER'S ACCOUNT

date	items	folio	debits	date	items	folio	credits
				5-31		CR-12	500-

FIGURE 3.10. (Continued.)

SUPPLIES EXPENSE

NATIONAL 17-459 WHITE 18-459 EYE-EASE LEDGER

date	items	folio	debits	date	items	folio	credits
				5-31		CR-12	20 —

FIGURE 3.10. (Continued.)

other journals. You'll use it to record depreciation expense and to record expense accruals when you prepare financial statements (see Chapter 11).

Figure 3.11 illustrates a typical page in a General Journal. Each entry must include the date the entry is made, the accounts being debited and credited, the amounts of the entry, and a reason for the entry. At the end of each month, any General Journal entries made should be posted to the General Ledger, indicating the General Journal page as the source of the entry.

SUMMING UP

In this chapter you saw that a Cash Receipts Journal and Cash Disbursements Journal should be used to record the daily flow of money in and out of your business checking account. Other transactions, such as the loss from a bad debt, are recorded in the General Journal.

Once a month these journals should be totaled, and the totals posted to the General Ledger, which will consist of all the T-accounts applicable to your business: Cash, Sales, Salaries Expense, Rent Expense, Utilities Expense, etc.

If you sell merchandise or services on credit, see Chapter 6 to find out how

GENERAL JOURNAL Page 1

	date	description	debit ①	credit ②
1	7 16	Bad Debt Expense	100 -	
2		Cash		100 -
3		to write off bad		
4		check from D. Dewald		
5				
6				
7				
8				
9				
10				
11				
12				
13				
14				
15				

FIGURE 3.11. General Journal entry made to write off a bad debt. Always list the account to be debited (Bad Debt Expense) first, then the account to be credited (Cash).

to invoice your customers, keep a sales journal, write up credit memos, post to general and subsidiary ledgers, and prepare a trial balance of your accounts receivable.

If you have a retail business, see Chapter 12 on procedures for recording inventories and cost of goods sold. If you are a manufacturer, see Chapter 13 on accounting for manufacturing expenses.

4

Cash

The accounting for cash is one of the most important accounting functions of any organization. Most transactions of a business are first recorded in the Cash Receipts and Cash Disbursements Journals. If these books aren't accurate, your financial statements won't be accurate. Since your cash balance is verifiable with an independent source (your bank), the reconciliation of your cash balance is your primary opportunity to detect errors in your records.

SEPARATION OF BUSINESS CASH

It's important that you keep your business cash completely separate from your personal cash. When you invest money in your business, you should deposit it in the business bank account and enter it in the Owner's Account column in the Cash Receipts Journal. If you draw money out of the business, this should be a debit to the Owner's Account made via the Cash Disbursements Journal.

CASH RECEIPTS JOURNAL

Chapter 3 describes how all receipts deposited in the business' bank account should be entered in the Cash Receipts Journal. Figure 3.9 illustrates a typical Cash Receipts Journal. If your business has more than one bank account, you should set up separate "amount" columns for each bank account.

CASH DISBURSEMENTS JOURNAL

The Cash Disbursements Journal is your detailed record of all checks written from your business bank account. Figure 3.4 illustrates a typical Cash Disbursements Journal. As with Cash Receipts, if you have more than one bank account for your business, separate "total" columns should be set up for each account.

BANK CHARGES AND CREDITS

You may receive notices from your bank that it has charged or credited your account for various reasons. For example, if a check you deposited to your account should be returned because of insufficient funds, your bank will debit your account (reduce your balance). You can record this either by adding the amount to your Cash Disbursements Journal or recording a journal entry in the General Journal, as illustrated in Figure 3.11. Routine bank charges such as the monthly service charge should be recorded in the Cash Disbursements Journal since this is easier than writing a journal entry.

GENERAL LEDGER CASH ACCOUNT

You should set up a Cash account in your General Ledger for each bank account your business has. Each month this account will be updated with postings from the Cash Receipts, Cash Disbursements, and General Journals. The cash balance in your General Ledger should be reconciled to the monthly bank statement as soon as you receive the statement.

RECONCILING THE MONTHLY BANK STATEMENT

At the end of each month, after you have entered all the month's cash transactions in the Cash Receipts and Cash Disbursements Journals you should reconcile your cash balance to the bank's balance in your checking account. Figure 4.1 illustrates how you should set up your bank reconciliation. Following are the steps you should follow to reconcile the bank statement to your General Ledger Cash account.

STEP 1. Make sure that for every item on the bank statement, you have received a matching cancelled check or debit or credit slip. If you find any errors, notify the bank immediately. The bank may not send copies of deposit slips with the statement, but you can match deposits with the duplicate slips you received when the deposits were made.

STEP 2. Make sure you have recorded all bank charges in the cash disbursements book and that all bank credit and debit slips have been recorded in the Cash Disbursements, Cash Receipts, or General Journals.

STEP 3. Determine the book (General Ledger) balance as of the reconciliation date (4/30/96 in the example). If you have already posted the General Ledger for the month (that is, entered all totals from the Journals) you can start out with the General Ledger Cash balance as of 4/30/96. We suggest, however, that you reconcile your bank statement before posting the General Ledger. This way any errors you find in the Journals can be corrected before the General Ledger is posted.

SCHEDULE	
PREPARED BY	DATE
REVIEWED BY	

Bank Statement Reconciliation
April 30, 1996

Book balance 3/31/96			3420.09
Plus april cash receipts			25037.54
Less april disbursements			(26163.89)
General journal entries to cash			-0-
Book balance 4-30-96			2293.74
Plus: outstanding checks			
	# 2054	20.42	
	2067	105.27	
	2068	50.34	
	2071	182.95	
	2075	10.52	
	2078	9.87	
	2091	35.46	
	2092	205.42	
	2096	10.98	
	2111	18.34	
	2113	106.72	
	2118	120.34	
	2128	87.68	
	2130	125.43	
		1089.74	1089.74
Less: deposits in transit			
	4-29	345.67	
	4-30	287.42	
		633.09	(633.09)
BANK BALANCE 4-30-96			2750.39

FIGURE 4.1. A completed bank reconciliation.

If you prepare the bank reconciliation before posting the General Ledger you will have to start out with the prior month's cash balance (line 1 on Figure 4.1) which should agree with the General Ledger. Then add the month's Cash Receipts and deduct the month's Cash Disbursements, and add or subtract any entries to the Cash account made via the General Journal to give you the month-end book balance (line 5 of Figure 4.1).

STEP 4. Add up outstanding checks. These are checks you wrote, recorded in Cash Disbursements and therefore deducted from your book balance, but which haven't yet been processed by the bank. You therefore have to add them back to your balance to arrive at the bank's balance. To determine which checks are outstanding, first arrange the cancelled checks in numerical sequence. Then match and check off cancelled checks with the previous month's outstanding checklist and the current month's Cash Disbursements Journal. The current month's outstanding checklist should consist of any checks not marked off on either the prior month's outstanding checklist or the current month's Cash Disbursements Journal.

STEP 5. Deposits outstanding are cash receipts that you recorded in your Cash Receipts Journal but, because you didn't deposit them in the bank by the end of the month, haven't yet been credited to your account. These amounts have to be deducted from your book balance to arrive at the bank's balance of your Cash account. You should match each deposit recorded in your Cash Receipts Journal with the bank's deposits listed in the statement. Any deposits (for that month) not recorded by the bank should be listed as deposits outstanding.

STEP 6. Add outstanding checks and deduct deposits outstanding from your book balance and it *should* agree with the bank balance. If it does not, you've made a mistake somewhere. Here are some suggestions for finding your errors:

(a) Double check all your figures in the reconciliation.
(b) Re-add the outstanding checks.
(c) Make sure you *added* the outstanding checks and *subtracted* the deposits in transit.
(d) Make sure you matched all the bank's cancelled checks and deposits to the receipts and disbursements books correctly.
(e) Make sure every item on the bank statement was entered in the books.
(f) Re-add the cash receipts and cash disbursements journals.
(g) If you *still* can't find your error, put it aside and try again tomorrow. Maybe the error will hit you in the face.

RECONCILING CASH BALANCE TO CHECKBOOK

Your checkbook is probably where you keep track of daily cash balances. It's obviously important that your running total be correct. The balance in your checkbook should agree with the balance in the General Ledger which has been reconciled to the bank statement. If it doesn't, first re-add all entries since your last reconciliation. If you still have a difference you should match your checkbook entries against the Cash Disbursements and Cash Receipts Journals to find and correct your error.

CHANGE FUND

If you make change in your daily business transactions with customers, it's a good idea to keep a change fund for each cash register or cash box. This should be a set amount of cash left in the register at the end of each day.

Suppose you decide to have a change fund of $50.00. You would then cash a check for $50.00, listing it in your Cash Disbursements Journal as a debit to a Change Fund account in your General Ledger. At the end of each day (or whenever you make deposits), you deposit all but the $50.00 in the bank. When making up financial statements, you add this $50.00 to the amount in the Cash account in your General Ledger to get your total cash.

If you decide to increase your change fund, or get another register, simply repeat the above process: Write and cash a check for the desired amount, enter it in your Cash Disbursements Journal, and debit it to a Change fund account in your General Ledger.

PETTY CASH FUND

A petty cash fund is useful for most businesses. It allows you to pay cash for miscellaneous small items without writing a check. For example, you might use petty cash for postage, emergency office supplies, or expenses such as transportation.

When setting up a cash fund, a good procedure is as follows: Get a cash box with a key and put one person in charge of it; write and cash a check for the desired fund amount, say, $100.00; record this check in your Cash Disbursements Journal; and debit it to a Petty Cash Fund account in your General Ledger.

Each time you spend the money in your petty cash box, you should fill out a slip as shown in Figure 4.2 stating which expense account is to be charged. Keep these slips in the cash box and when the cash gets low, total up all the slips and write a check for this amount. Then cash this check, put the cash in the box and when entering the check in your Cash Disbursements Journal, summarize the various expenses that will be charged (see Figure 4.3).

When preparing financial statements, the $100 in the petty cash fund is added to the debit balance in the Cash and Change Fund accounts to get your total cash figure. This $100 debit balance in your Petty Cash Fund account in the General Ledger will remain on your books as is until you increase or decrease your petty cash fund.

No. 14 Amount $ 3 50/00

RECEIVED OF PETTY CASH

12/8 19 96

For Stamps

Charge to Postage Expense

F. Campbell — Approved by

Rob Smith — Received by

EFFICIENCY® LINE No. 2685 AN **AMPAD** PRODUCT

FIGURE 4.2. How to fill out a petty cash slip.

CASH DISBURSEMENTS JOURNAL Page 2

	date	payee	① check#	② total	③ accounts payable	④ salaries	⑤ general	⑥ gen. acct name
1	2 14	Petty Cash	1035	84 -			34	Owner's Ex
2							26	Postage Ex
3							24	Misc. Ex
4								
5								
6								
7								
8								
9								
10								
11								
12								
13								
14								
15								
16								
17								
18								
19								
20								

FIGURE 4.3. Cash Disbursements entry illustrating itemization of petty cash reimbursement.

SUMMING UP

Reconciling your General Ledger Cash account with the monthly bank statement is one of the most important accounting functions. This is how you'll find any errors you may have made in posting or totaling cash receipts and disbursements.

A change fund is useful for retail or service businesses that make change daily in customer transactions. When depositing each day's receipts in the bank, leave the change fund intact in the register or cash box.

A petty cash fund will provide cash for small miscellaneous expenditures. You should fill out a petty cash slip each time money is spent; replenish the fund when it gets low; and summarize the slips and enter appropriate expense charges in the Cash Disbursements Journal when you write a replacement check.

5

Purchases and Accounts Payable

The purchasing function is a very importatnt part of your business. If you're not careful, you may end up losing money by (1) ordering merchandise you don't need; (2) accepting merchandise you haven't ordered; (3) paying for goods you haven't received; and (4) paying higher prices than you have agreed to.

By keeping careful records, as discussed below, you can avoid the above mistakes. But smart purchasing involves a lot more than careful recordkeeping. In a retail operation, for example, purchasing the wrong merchandise could be disastrous. If the goods sit in your store unsold, you will end up taking a loss.

In a manufacturing business, it's the purchases of raw materials and parts which are critical to the business' success. In a mail order business, it's the mailing lists, advertising, and printing which might make or break the business.

In any business, purchasing the right product or service at the right price (and the right terms) is a key ingredient in the success of the business. Money saved in purchasing is money you can add directly to profits. And vice versa, money lost because of poor purchasing comes directly *out* of profits.

While it's beyond the scope of this book to go into the specifics of making purchasing decisions, we *will* cover methods for keeping control over and accounting for purchases you make.

PURCHASE ORDERS

Whichever method you use to record purchases, the first step to keeping track of monies spent on supplies, raw materials, finished goods, etc., is to use numbered purchase order forms (See Figure 5.1). By ordering *everything* through purchase orders you'll have better control. For example, you'll

purchase order

TRIP

PURCHASE ORDER

No. 3615

To

Address

City

Ship To

Date ______ 19___

For

Req. No.

How Ship

Date Required

Terms

	QUANTITY ORDERED	RECEIVED	PLEASE SUPPLY ITEMS LISTED BELOW	PRICE	UNIT
1					
2					
3					
4					
5					
6					

IMPORTANT

OUR ORDER NUMBER MUST APPEAR ON ALL INVOICES, PACKAGES, ETC.
PLEASE NOTIFY US IMMEDIATELY IF YOU ARE UNABLE TO SHIP COMPLETE ORDER BY DATE SPECIFIED.

Please Send ______ Copies Of Your Invoice With Original Bill Of Lading

Purchasing Agent

1S 144 Rediform®
Poly Pak (50 sets) 1P 144

ORIGINAL

FIGURE 5.1. A purchase order form that can be ordered from the suppliers listed in Chapter 18.

know on what date you ordered an item, the quantity, the price, and so forth. It gives your supplier complete information about what you want, when you want it, and how you want it shipped. When you receive the order, you can check to see that what you got is what you ordered.

Purchase order forms are available in various layouts, in carbon sets, and can be imprinted with your name and address. It's best to get forms that are consecutively numbered. That way you can keep a numerical file of all orders. The original purchase order goes to the supplier and you will need one or more copies for your records. Forms are available at your local office supply store or can be ordered from the suppliers listed in Chapter 18.

Figure 5.2 is an example of how to fill out a purchase order form. Your company name and address should be typed or printed at the top. The supplier's name and address appears after "to." After "ship to," write in

PURCHASE ORDER

JONES BAKERY
110 Main Street
Anywhere, U.S.A. 10000

No. 3616

Date June 1 19 97

For

To Zippy Box Co.

Req. No.

Address 666 Main St.

How Ship UPS

City Anywhere, U.S.A. 10000

Date Required June 20th

Ship To above

Terms COD

	QUANTITY ORDERED	QUANTITY RECEIVED	PLEASE SUPPLY ITEMS LISTED BELOW	PRICE		UNIT
1	500		#348 cake boxes	8	00	100
2	1000		#252 donut boxes	7	50	100
3						
4						
5						
6						

IMPORTANT
OUR ORDER NUMBER MUST APPEAR ON ALL INVOICES, PACKAGES, ETC.
PLEASE NOTIFY US IMMEDIATELY IF YOU ARE UNABLE TO SHIP COMPLETE ORDER BY DATE SPECIFIED.

Please Send 2 Copies Of Your Invoice With Original Bill Of Lading

Kathy Jones
Purchasing Agent

ORIGINAL

1S 144 Rediform®
Poly Pak (50 sets) 1P 144

FIGURE 5.2. A purchase order filled out by Kathy Jones of Jones Bakery.

"above" or list your shipping address if it's different from your address at the top of the form (you may have a warehouse or stores at different locations).

The date is the date on which you place the order. "For" and "requisition number" were left blank in this example. After "how ship" you list UPS, parcel post, or the name of a trucking company, unless you want to leave the shipping method up to the supplier. After "date required" put the date on which you want the goods delivered.

"Terms" will usually be up to the supplier unless you're an important customer. You may have to send a check with your order (cash terms) if you're a new customer and haven't established a credit rating. An alternative is "C.O.D.," which stands for "Cash on Delivery." In this case you pay for the goods when you receive them. However, once you establish a good credit rating or a reputation with your supplier, you may be able to purchase merchandise on credit. "Net 30 days," for example, would allow you 30 days to pay for the merchandise after you receive it. Some suppliers offer discounts for early payment, such as "2% 10 net 30." This means if you pay within 10 days you can take two percent off the invoice total; otherwise you must pay the whole amount within 30 days.

Note that in the sample purchase order there's a column to list the quantity ordered and the quantity received. This allows you to compare the amount received against the amount ordered when the goods arrive. By listing the price on the purchase order, you alert the supplier as to what you expect to pay. If prices have gone up, the supplier should notify you of the change before shipping your order.

KEEPING TRACK OF PURCHASES

You'll find below three methods for handling your company's purchases. Method 1 is for all companies that keep their records on the cash basis of accounting. If you're on the accrual basis, you can use either method 2 or method 3.

Method 1: Cash Method

If you're on the cash basis of accounting for income tax purposes (as discussed in Chapters 2 and 3), you'll record expenses at the time you pay them. This will be done via the Cash Disbursements Journal, as described in Chapter 3. See Figure 5.3 for an illustration of expenses recorded in the Cash Disbursements Journal.

Method 2: Simplified Accrual Method

Under the simplified accrual method you can first record your expenses in the Cash Disbursements Journal as you would if you were on the cash basis of accounting, but you must make adjustments to your records to reflect goods and services received but not paid for. At the end of every fiscal year (the end of the business' accounting year for tax purposes) you must make an adjustment for all unpaid invoices for goods and services received.

To make this end-of-the-year adjustment, collect all the outstanding invoices (bills) for goods received but not paid for. Enter these in your General Journal as debits to the applicable expense accounts and credits to Accounts Payable. Then post to your General Ledger accounts. Now your General Ledger accounts will accurately reflect the status of your purchases on an accrual basis.

Let's look at a sample situation. The XYZ Company owes $14,500 to vari-

45-164 EYE-EASE
45-464 20/20 BUFF

CASH DISBURSEMENTS JOURNAL

Page 2

	date		payee	check#	total	salar.	rent	printing	off.sup.	fuel	general	gen. acct. name
				1	2	3	4	5	6	7	8	9
1	3	6	Office Supply Corp.	2034	54				54			
2	3	10	Jiffy Printers	2035	120			120				
3	3	15	Easy Gas	2036	25					25		
4												
5												
6												
7												
8												
9												
10												
11												
12												
13												
14												
15												
16												
17												
18												
19												
20												

FIGURE 5.3. Page from a Cash Disbursements Journal showing the recording of payments for several purchases.

ous suppliers for goods received as of December 31, 1997. An itemization is as follows:

Invoice from	For	In amount of
ABC Co.	Raw materials	$6,000.00
DEF Co.	Packaging supplies	1,300.00
GHI Co.	Raw materials	7,200.00

Before preparing financial statements for the year, this $14,500 should be entered in the General Journal as illustrated in Figure 5.4. These entries are then posted in the General Ledger accounts as shown in Figure 5.5. Note that $13,200 is debited to Raw Materials Expense, $1,300 is debited to Packaging Supplies Expense, and the total $14,500 is credited to Accounts Payable. The expense accounts will be cleared after the financial statements are done (see Chapter 11 on Financial Statements). The entries should then be reversed, crediting Raw Materials Expense with $13,200, crediting Packaging Supplies Expense with $1,300, and debiting Accounts Payable with $14,500 (which makes the Accounts Payable balance zero). In the new year the procedure would be the same as for the prior year. When the ABC Company is paid, it

GENERAL JOURNAL — Page 12

	date	description	debit	credit
1	12-31	Raw Material expense	13200 –	
2		Packaging supplies expense	1300 –	
3		Accounts payable		14500 –
4		to record open invoices to:		
5		ABC Co. $6,000		
6		DEF Co. 1,300		
7		GHI Co. 7,200		
8				
9				
10				
11				
12				
13				
14				
15				

FIGURE 5.4. Entries in this General Journal page have been posted to the General Ledger accounts in Figure 5.5.

RAW MATERIALS EXPENSE

date	items	folio	debits	date	items	folio	credits
12-31		GJ-12	13200 —				

PACKAGING SUPPLIES EXPENSE

date	items	folio	debits	date	items	folio	credits
12-31		GJ-12	1300 —				

ACCOUNTS PAYABLE

date	items	folio	debits	date	items	folio	credits
				12-31		GJ-12	145 00

FIGURE 5.5. Entries in these General Ledger accounts have been taken from the General Journal page in Figure 5.4.

will be listed in the Cash Disbursements Journal and debited to Raw Materials Expense.

Method 3: Accrual Method

If you have a relatively large accounts payable (money you owe to suppliers for goods received but not yet paid for) and want to keep a record of how much you owe (and to whom) on a daily basis, the straight accrual method may be best for you. This is how it works.

Set up a Purchases Journal as shown in Figure 5.6. Record invoices from suppliers daily as they're received, listing the date of invoice, invoice number, the supplier's name, and the total amount. The dollar amount is written in again under the proper column heading. In some cases one invoice may cover two different expenses such as Office Supplies Expense and Printing Expense. Figure 5.6 illustrates several typical entries.

At the end of the month, total the columns in your Purchases Journal and post to your General Ledger accounts. The amount from the "total" column will be credited to Accounts Payable as shown in Figure 5.7. The other totals should be debited to the applicable expense accounts. Each item in the "general" column will have to be posted individually to its proper expense account. You should check off each item as you post it with a red check mark to avoid duplicate posting. Note that "PJ–3" was written under "folio" on each account in Figure 5.7 to show where the information was obtained.

When you pay invoices, record the payment as usual in your Cash Disbursements Journal, which should have a column called "Accounts Payable" as shown in Figure 5.8. At the end of the month, total the Accounts Payable column in your Cash Disbursements Journal and debit the amount to Accounts Payable in your General Ledger (see Figure 5.9 for example).

ACCOUNTS PAYABLE SUBSIDIARY LEDGER

If you use the strict accrual method of accounting for purchases (method 3), you should set up a subsidiary ledger for each supplier you deal with. This allows you to see at a glance how much you owe each one and when payments are due. It gives you a complete record of all business conducted with a supplier. A typical subsidiary ledger should be set up as shown in Figure 5.10.

At the end of the month *credit* the entries from your Purchases Journal in the applicable Subsidiary Ledger account; then *debit* entries from your Cash Disbursements Journal. The difference between credits and debits gives you your credit balance, or the amount you now owe each supplier. The Subsidiary Ledger account in Figure 5.10 shows several months' entries. Note that

PURCHASES JOURNAL Page 3

date	Supplier	Inv. #	Total	Raw Material	Freight	Small Tools	General Account	General Amount
	Balance from previous page		3736 -	3590 -	76 -	70 -		-0-
2-25	Barnard Supply	3042	520 -	500 -	20 -			
2-27	Elco Office Co.	123	150 -				Off. Supp. Ex.	100 - ✓
							Printing Ex.	50 - ✓
2-30	Elgin Tool Co.	70005	84 -		4 -	80 -		
			4490 - ✓	4090 - ✓	100 - ✓	150 - ✓		150 - ✓

FIGURE 5.6. Page from a Purchases Journal showing several entries for purchases. Items are listed in the Purchases Journal as invoices are received.

ACCOUNTS PAYABLE

date	items	folio	debits	date	items	folio	credits
				2·28		PJ-3	4490 -

RAW MATERIALS EXPENSE

date	items	folio	debits	date	items	folio	credits
2·28		PJ-3	4090 -				

FIGURE 5.7. Entries in these General Ledger accounts were taken from the Purchases Journal in Figure 5.6. Note that Accounts Payable is credited and the expense accounts are debited.

FREIGHT EXPENSE

date	items	folio	debits	date	items	folio	credits
2-28		PJ-3	100 -				

SMALL TOOLS EXPENSE

date	items	folio	debits	date	items	folio	credits
2-28		PJ-3	150 -				

FIGURE 5.7. (Continued.)

OFFICE SUPPLIES EXPENSE

date	items	folio	debits	date	items	folio	credits
2-28		PJ-3	100-				

PRINTING EXPENSE

date	items	folio	debits	date	items	folio	credits
2-28		PJ-3	50-				

FIGURE 5.7. (Continued.)

CASH DISBURSEMENTS JOURNAL Page 5

	date		payee	① check#	② total	③ accts. payable	④ salar.	⑤ general	⑥ gen acct name
1	3	1	G. Smith	2043	200		200		
2	3	3	JKL Co.	2044	350	350			
3			MNO Co.	2045	870	870			
4	3	12	Ecco Bldg. Co.	2046	400			400	Rent Ex.
5	3	15	PQR Co.	2047	972	972			
6									
7									
8									
9									
10									
11									
12									
13									
14									
15									
16									
17									
18									
19									
20									

FIGURE 5.8. When payments are made to suppliers, list in the Accounts Payable column of Cash Disbursements Journal.

ACCOUNTS PAYABLE

DATE 19__		ITEMS	FOLIO	√	DEBITS	DATE 19__		ITEMS	FOLIO	√	CREDITS
3	31	March Payments	CD-5		4050	* 2	28	Feb. Purchases	PJ-3		4540
		*Prior entry									

FIGURE 5.9. When posting to General Ledger from Cash Disbursements Journal, debit Accounts Payable for payments made to suppliers.

ABC Co.
100 Main St.
Anywhere, USA

	date	invoice or check#	① debit	② credit	③ credit balance	④ folio
1	1 31	2054		(a) 540	540	PJ-1
2		2067		(b) 310	850	PJ-1
3	2 28	628	(a) 540			CD-3
4		3079		(b) 770	1080	PJ-2
5	3 31	3185		250		PJ-3
6		670	(b) 1080		250	CD-4
7						
8						
9						
10						
11						
12						
13						
14						
15						
16						
17						
18						
19						
20						
21						
22						
23						
24						
25						
26						
27						

FIGURE 5.10. An Accounts Payable subsidiary ledger page for the ABC Company. All invoices and payments are posted from the Purchases Journal and the Cash Disbursements Journal. The credit balance is what is owed the supplier. If there's a debit balance, put brackets around the amount when you enter it in the "credit balance" column.

payments (debits) are keyed to the invoices they cover. Check 628 was a payment for Invoice 2054, so they are both keyed with an (a). Check 670 was a payment for Invoices 2067 and 3079, all keyed with a (b). You should check off entries in the Purchases Journal and Cash Disbursements Journal as you post them to the subsidiary ledger in order to avoid duplicate entries.

RETURNS AND REFUNDS

Sometimes you'll receive damaged or wrong merchandise, or an order may be short. Whatever the cause, you should contact your supplier and request a cash refund or a credit memo which allows you to deduct the amount from your next payment. If your supplier sends a cash refund, you can treat it as any other cash receipt—that is, record the amount in your Cash Receipts Journal as illustrated in Chapter 3, Figure 3.9. At the end of the month, credit the applicable expense account in your General Ledger as illustrated in Chapter 3, Figure 3.10.

If you use method 1 or 2 to record purchases, you should handle credit memos as follows: Deduct the amount of the Credit Memo from your next payment to the supplier. For example, if the invoice you wish to pay is for $150 and the Credit Memo is for $15, you pay the amount of $135. Record the $135 as usual in your Cash Disbursements Journal.

If you're using method 3 for recording purchases, handle Credit Memos as follows: Record them in your Purchases Journal as shown in Figure 5.11. Note that a bracket is put around the amount to indicate it should be subtracted when computing totals. At the end of the month, list the Credit Memo amount as a *debit* in the supplier's Subsidiary Ledger account (see Figure 5.12).

TRIAL BALANCE

Periodically you should take a trial balance of the subsidiary ledger. Make a list of all suppliers, entering the balances from your subsidiary ledger. The total of all balances should match the balance in your Accounts Payable account (credits minus debits). Figure 5.13 illustrates a trial balance showing a credit balance that matches the balance in the Accounts Payable account.

If your totals don't match, first recheck your figuring, then go back to your Cash Disbursements Journal and make sure that every applicable item is checked off, indicating it has been posted to the subsidiary ledger. You should check especially that refunds were posted properly. The same procedure should be followed with your Purchases Journal. Finally, you should check individual arithmetic on subsidiary ledger accounts.

SUMMING UP

A purchase order form should be filled out each time you make a purchase or place an order for supplies, raw materials, finished goods, etc. Keeping these orders filed numerically gives better control. You should also check incoming shipments against them for accuracy.

PURCHASES JOURNAL Page 4

18-408 EYE EASE LEDGER

	date	supplier	Inv. # (1)	total (2)	raw mat (3)	freight (4)	general (5)	gen acct name (6)
1	3 20	DAF Co.	CM/004	(13)	(13)			
2								
3								
4								
5								
6								
7								
8								
9								
10								
11								
12								
13								
14								
15								
16								
17								
18								
19								
20								

FIGURE 5.11. Illustration showing how to record a Credit Memo in Purchases Journal. The brackets around the $13 mean it will be debited to subsidiary ledger and subtracted from total purchases credited to Accounts Payable.

DEF Co.
200 Main St.
Anywhere, USA

18-408 EYE EASE LEDGER

	date		invoice or check #		① debit	② credit	③ credit balance	④ folio
1	3	31	CM 1004		13			PJ-4

FIGURE 5.12. Subsidiary ledger illustrating the entry of a Credit Memo. Note that the $13 is listed as a debit.

TRIAL BALANCE AS OF 6/30/96

Supplier	*Credit Balance*
ABC COMPANY	$ 230.00
DEF COMPANY	50.00
GHI COMPANY	(15.00)
JKL COMPANY	340.00
MNO COMPANY	—
PQR COMPANY	150.00
STU COMPANY	—
VWX COMPANY	520.00
	$1,275.00

FIGURE 5.13. Trial balance of Accounts Payable and General Ledger Accounts Payable account. (Continued on next page.)

ACCOUNTS PAYABLE

DATE 19__		ITEMS	FOLIO	√	DEBITS	DATE 19__		ITEMS	FOLIO	√	CREDITS
1	31	Jan. Payments	CD-2		670	1	31	Jan. Purchases	PJ-1		540
2	28	Feb. "	CD-4		350	2	28	Feb. "	PJ-2		980
3	30	Mar. "	CD-6		500	3	30	Mar. "	PJ-2		1250
4	30	Apr. "	CD-7		1000	4	30	Apr. "	PJ-3		1050
5	31	May. "	CD-9		925	5	31	May. "	PJ-4		875
6	30	Jun. "	CD-11		925	6	30	Jun. "	PJ-4		950
					4370						5645
											− 4370
											1275

FIGURE 5.13. (Continued.)

You will want to use method 1 if you are on the cash basis of accounting for tax purposes. Method 2 or 3 can be used for accrual systems. If you use method 3, you'll probably want to set up an Accounts Payable subsidiary ledger. A trial balance of this ledger should be periodically taken and reconciled to your Accounts Payable account.

You should ask for a refund or credit memo when a shipment is short or damaged, and remember to subtract rather than add credit memo amounts on your Purchases Journal and to record them as *debits* on your subsidiary ledger.

6

Sales and Accounts Receivable

This chapter will show you how to invoice your customers, keep a sales journal, write up credit memos, post to general and subsidiary ledgers, and prepare a trial balance of your accounts receivable. The accounts receivable section of this chapter is not applicable to businesses that sell for cash only (do not give credit to their customers).

INVOICES

When you sell services or merchandise to a customer, you'll send them a bill or invoice similar to the sample shown in Figure 6.1. The basic purpose of the invoice is to inform the customer when and how goods were shipped; to tell the customer how much is owed, and when and under what terms it's due; and to provide a record for you.

Invoices such as the one shown are available at most office supply stores, or can be ordered from the suppliers listed in Chapter 18. It's important to get consecutively numbered invoice forms because that makes it easier to keep track of orders shipped and monies received. These forms are available in carboned sets that provide an original plus as many copies as you may need. Your customers may require two copies of an invoice, in which case you'll send them the original and a second copy. You'll need two copies for your own files—one to be kept in a consecutively numbered file and another for your customer files. If you have sales representatives, they will need a copy. The last copy of the invoice form, marked "packing slip," can be inserted in the carton of merchandise when it's shipped.

Figure 6.2 is an example of how an invoice might be filled out. The invoice date should be the date merchandise was shipped or picked up by the customer, or the date the service was rendered by your company. Under "sold to," list the name and *billing* address of your customer. Under "shipped to," list the shipping address, if different. Otherwise type in "same."

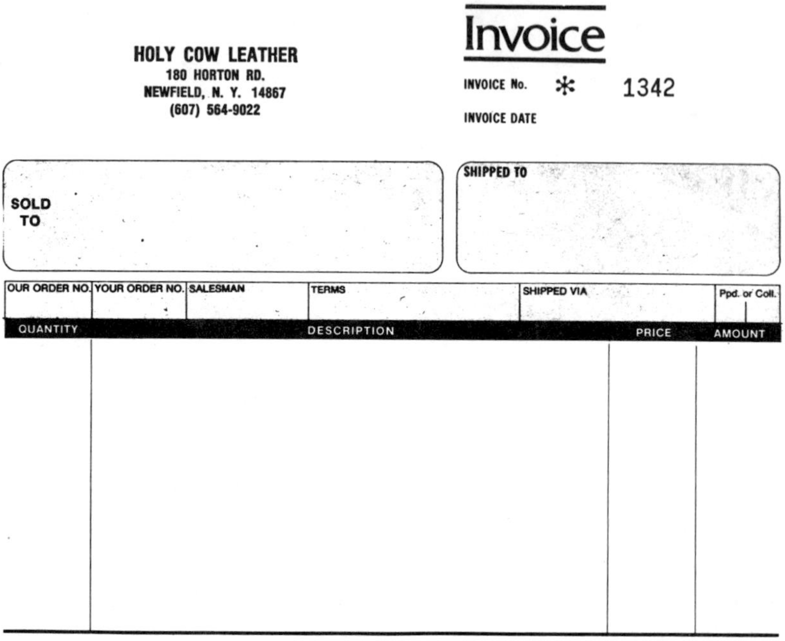
HOLY COW LEATHER
180 HORTON RD.
NEWFIELD, N. Y. 14867
(607) 564-9022

Invoice

INVOICE No. * 1342
INVOICE DATE

SOLD TO

SHIPPED TO

OUR ORDER NO.	YOUR ORDER NO.	SALESMAN	TERMS	SHIPPED VIA	Ppd. or Coll.

QUANTITY	DESCRIPTION	PRICE	AMOUNT

FIGURE 6.1. Standard invoice form, available in consecutively numbered carbon sets and imprinted with company's name and address.

Under "our order no.," list the number from your own company's order form. Under "your order no.," list the number given on a written order from the customer, if there is one. If a sales representative or company salesperson made the order, list his or her name under "salesman."

Under "terms," list your company's standard payment terms. "Net 30 days" means the invoice must be paid in full within 30 days of the invoice date. "1% 10 net 30" means the customer may deduct one percent of the invoice total if it is paid within 10 days; otherwise the full amount is due within 30 days. "3% 10 EOM" means the customer may deduct three percent from the total and pay the bill by the 10th of the following month. Whatever terms you use should be agreed to in advance by you and your customer.

Under "shipped via," list the carrier (parcel post, United Parcel Service, name of trucking company, etc.) if there was one. If the order was prepaid, check the box marked "Ppd." or type "prepaid" under "terms." If the invoice is to be collected on delivery, check the box marked "coll.," or type "collect" or "C.O.D." under "terms."

The bottom half of the invoice provides space to list the quantity of each

HOLY COW LEATHER
180 HORTON RD.
NEWFIELD, N. Y. 14867
(607) 564-9022

Invoice

INVOICE No. * 1337

INVOICE DATE 3/1/96

SOLD TO	SHIPPED TO
TOPSY TOY CO. 100 Main St. Orange, New York 10000	TOPSY TOY CO. Warehouse 105 Main St. Orange, N.Y. 10000

OUR ORDER NO.	YOUR ORDER NO.	SALESMAN	TERMS	SHIPPED VIA	Ppd. or Coll.
52035	XL100035	Jones	1% 10 net 30	UPS	

QUANTITY	DESCRIPTION	PRICE	AMOUNT
6 gross	keyrings, #52, imprinted	$ 5/gr	30.00
10 gross	wallets, #304, imprinted	20/gr	200.00
8 gross	billfolds, #305, imprinted		B.O.
			$230.00
	UPS charges		1.35
			$231.35

FIGURE 6.2. Completed invoice, ready to send to the customer.

item shipped, a description, a unit price, and the total amount. This space is used for listing sales taxes and shipping charges, if any. In the example shown, "B.O." was typed under "amount" for the third item; "B.O." stands for "back order." Although this item was on the customer's order, it was out of stock at the time and was therefore back ordered. Note that no price and amount are listed for this item. It will be invoiced separately when it's shipped. Some customers will not allow back orders and either will want you to wait and ship the whole order at once, or will simply cancel any items you don't have in stock.

Processing Invoices. Invoices should be typed and sent to customers as soon as possible after orders are shipped—either the same day or at most the following day. Then one copy should be filed in a Sales folder for that month—that is, January Sales, February Sales, etc. These should be filed in numerical sequence so you can keep track of all orders. If a mistake is made in typing an invoice form, a copy should be marked "void" and kept in the monthly sales file so you know an invoice for that number is not missing.

You may want to maintain separate folders for the invoices of each customer in order to see at a glance what you've sold to each account. If you do this, another copy of the invoice is filed in the customer's file. For example, if you send an invoice to the Topsy Toy Company on March 3, file one copy of the invoice in the March Sales folder and another in the Topsy Toy Company folder.

SALES JOURNAL

A Sales Journal is your permanent record of a period's sales. If you wish to break down your sales by product line or department, a Sales Journal is the place to do this. Figure 6.3 is an example of a page from a typical Sales Journal. Note that invoice numbers are listed consecutively and that some customers have purchased items from several departments on one order.

At the end of each month you should take that month's Sales folder and copy the information from the invoices into your Sales Journal. If weekly information is desired, weekly subtotals are written on the Sales Journal.

SALES JOURNAL Page 3

	date		customer name	① inv. #	② Dept. A	③ Dept. B	④ Dept. C	⑤ invoice total
1	3	25	Mark III Co.	1005	50 -			50 -
2			Topsy Toy Co.	1006		250 -	75 -	325 -
3			Hudson Soap	1007		350 -		350 -
4			Madison Gift	1008	200 -			200 -
5	3	26	Lewis & Son	1009	150 -	35 -	180 -	365 -
6			Mannix Co.	1010		25 -		25 -
7			Solothon Corp.	1011	600 -		500 -	1100 -
8								
9								
10								
11								
12								
13								
14								
15								
16								
17								
18								
19								
20								

FIGURE 6.3. Sample page from a Sales Journal, with sales recorded for three departments.

If you have an extra copy of all invoices available, you can use these for your permanent record of sales. Instead of writing every invoice into the Sales Journal, simply take an adding machine tape of all invoices billed during the month. If you have separate departments or products, take separate tapes, making sure that the individual departments' sale totals equals total sales. All tapes should be taken twice and totals matched to be sure you haven't made an error (this is standard procedure for any computing done in accounting). The adding machine tapes should then be stapled to the invoices as your permanent record of sales.

CREDIT MEMOS

From time to time it may be necessary to issue a credit memo to a customer because of overcharging, a merchandise return, price adjustments due to damage, and so forth. Figure 6.4 shows an example of a typical credit memo. Note that it's typed on an invoice form, with "CM" typed in front of the invoice number.

HOLY COW LEATHER
180 HORTON RD.
NEWFIELD, N. Y. 14867
(607) 564-9022

Invoice

INVOICE No. * CM 1340
INVOICE DATE 4/15/96

SOLD TO: Lewis & Son
505 Main St.
Charleston, W. Va. 20000

SHIPPED TO

OUR ORDER NO.	YOUR ORDER NO.	SALESMAN	TERMS	SHIPPED VIA	Ppd. or Coll.
		Smith			

QUANTITY	DESCRIPTION	PRICE	AMOUNT
3ea	#405 handbags -- returned - defective, no strap	$8 ea	($24.00)
	CREDIT MEMO		

FIGURE 6.4. Credit Memo issued to a customer for the return of defective merchandise.

Credit memos should be filed in the monthly Sales folder in numerical order with the invoices. When listing them on the Sales Journal, however, brackets should be placed around the amount, which should then be subtracted from the totals. Figure 6.5 illustrates the listing of a credit memo on a Sales Journal. If you use a copy of invoices and adding machine tapes as a permanent record of sales, be sure to *subtract* credit memos on the adding machine tape.

POSTING SALES TO GENERAL LEDGER

If your sales are strictly on a cash (no credit) basis, sales are recorded in the Cash Receipts Journal when the cash is deposited in the bank (see Figure 3.9 in Chapter 3). At the end of the month, total sales from the Cash Receipts Journal are posted to the General Ledger by crediting Sales (see Figure 3.10 in Chapter 3).

When selling on credit, however, you not only need to know what your total sales are, but also how much of this total amount has been paid and how much is still outstanding. Therefore you'll need an Accounts Receivable account.

Figure 6.6 shows the posting of monthly sales in the Sales and Accounts Receivable accounts. Note that sales are listed on the debit side of the Accounts

SALES JOURNAL Page 4

	date	customer name	① inv. #	② Dept. A	③ Dept. B	④ Dept. C	⑤ invoice total
1	3 30	Ronson Co.	1062		250-		250
2		Paper Prod. Corp.	1063	1050-		300-	1350
3		Topsy Toy Co.	CM 1064		(24)		(24)
4		Rubber Bubble	1065			840-	840
5							
6							
7							
8							
9							
10							
11							
12							
13							
14							

FIGURE 6.5. Sample page from a Sales Journal showing a Credit Memo listing.

SALES

date	items	folio	debits	date	items	folio	credits
				1-31		SF	9741 -
				2-28		SF	11842 -
				3-31		SF	14765 -

ACCOUNTS RECEIVABLE

date	items	folio	debits	date	items	folio	credits
1-31		SF	9741 -				
2-28		SF	11842 -				
3-31		SF	14765 -				

FIGURE 6.6. How to post monthly sales to the Sales and Accounts Receivable accounts in the General Ledger.

Receivable and the credit side of the Sales accounts. These monthly figures are taken from the adding machine tapes in the monthly Sales folders. Thus "SF" is listed under "folio" because "SF" stands for "Sales folder." If you record sales in a Sales Journal, you'll record sales in the General Ledger from the Sales Journal. Your "folio" reference will then be "SJ" for "Sales Journal."

If you record sales by department or product line, set up a General Ledger account for each department or product. Then post monthly total sales for each department or product line in its appropriate Sales account. See Figure 6.7 for an example of a company with two product lines. Note that sales are broken down into separate Sales accounts, but only one Accounts Receivable account is kept for total sales. "SJ-1, 2, 3," etc., are listed under "folio" to indicate the Sales Journal page the figures were taken from.

POSTING SALES TO SUBSIDIARY LEDGERS

A subsidiary ledger listing the debits, credits, and outstanding balance for each customer is valuable for providing more control over the credit extended each of your customers. By glancing at the ledger you can tell how often and what amounts they have purchased, the timeliness of their payments, and the present outstanding receivable. When a customer places a new order, you can immediately check their file to see if you should offer them continued credit. By looking through your subsidiary ledger periodically, you can see which customers have become inactive and thereby direct more sales effort toward them. The subsidiary ledger will also be used to prepare an aged trial balance.

Figure 6.8 illustrates a subsidiary ledger with sales posted. Post the sales information on your subsidiary ledger weekly or monthly from the invoices in your monthly Sales folder. The date on the subsidiary ledger sheet is the date of the invoice. The reference number is the invoice or credit memo number. Sales are listed under debit. Credit memos are listed under credit. The debit balance is the balance owed by the customer. If there's a credit balance due the customer, this would be listed with brackets around it in the debit balance column.

In order to be sure that every invoice is posted to the subsidiary ledger, put a check mark in the upper right-hand corner of each invoice as you post it to the subsidiary ledger. In order to be sure not to list an invoice twice, you should post the invoices in numerical order on the subsidiary ledger, just as you file them in the monthly Sales folders.

SALES: PRODUCT A

date	items	folio	debits	date	items	folio	credits
				1-30		SJ-1	8725 -
				2-28		SJ-2	6242 -
				3-31		SJ-3	9254 -

SALES: PRODUCT B

date	items	folio	debits	date	items	folio	credits
				1-30		SJ-1	10250 -
				2-28		SJ-2	12340 -
				3-31		SJ-3	11642 -

FIGURE 6.7 Posting of monthly sales from a Sales Journal for a company with two product lines.

ACCOUNTS RECEIVABLE

date	items	folio	debits	date	items	folio	credits
1-30		SJ-1	18975 -				
2-28		SJ-2	18582 -				
3-31		SJ-3	20896 -				

FIGURE 6.7. (Continued.)

TOPSY TOY CO.
100 Main Street
Orange, N.Y. 10000 Sales Rep: Marvin Jones

			①	②	③	④
	date	reference #	debit	credit	debit balance	
1	3 1	1314	231 35		231 35	
2	3 18	1342	506 -		737 35	
3	3 25	CM 1358		24 -	713 35	
4						
5						
6						
7						
8						
9						
10						
11						
12						
13						
14						
15						
16						
17						
18						
19						
20						

FIGURE 6.8. A subsidiary ledger sheet.

POSTING CASH RECEIPTS TO THE GENERAL LEDGER

When your customers pay their invoices, the checks you receive will be listed under Accounts Receivable in your Cash Receipts Journal (see Chapter 3). Figure 6.9 shows an example of a page in a Cash Receipts Journal listing several accounts receivable items. Note that this page is from the end of the month and totals have been made under the last entries in each column. The total cash received for the month should be posted to the debit side of the Cash account. The Accounts Receivable total is posted to the credit side of the Accounts Receivable account. This posting procedure is illustrated in Figure 6.10. The general items would be posted individually to the credit side of their applicable accounts, as discussed in Chapter 3.

CASH RECEIPTS JOURNAL Page 6

			1	2	3	4	5	6	
9-6				total	Cash	Accounts	general		
9-6	date	item	amount	deposit	Sales	Receivable	account	amount	
1		Balance from CR-5	11112 35			11012 35		100 -	1
2	2-26	Rubber Bubble	840 -			840 -			2
3		Paper Products Co.	1050 -			1050 -			3
4		Ronson Co.	250 -			250 -			4
5		U.S. Treasury	50 -	2190 -			Tax ex.	50 -	5
6	2-27	Bank	25 -				Int. Inc.	25 -	6
7		Madison Gift	200 -	225 -		200 -			7
8	2-28	Topsy Toy Co.	325 -			325 -			8
9		Lewis & Son	365 -			365 -			9
10		Amco Leather	35 -	725 -		35 -			10
11			14252 35			14077 35		175 -	11
12									12
13									13
14									14
15									15

FIGURE 6.9. Sample page from a Cash Receipts Journal showing several accounts receivable listings and monthly totals.

CASH

date	items	folio	debits	date	items	folio	credits
2-28		CR-6	14252 35				

ACCOUNTS RECEIVABLE

date	items	folio	debits	date	items	folio	credits
				2-28		CR-6	14077 35

FIGURE 6.10. Cash and Accounts Receivable accounts showing how to post cash receipts to the General Ledger.

POSTING CASH RECEIPTS TO THE SUBSIDIARY LEDGER

The accounts receivable items on the Cash Receipts Journal (Figure 6.9) should be posted weekly or monthly to your subsidiary ledger. After each item is posted, a red check mark should be placed next to the figure on the Cash Receipts Journal. This will insure that all items are posted only once.

Figure 6.11 illustrates a subsidiary ledger with cash receipts posted. The data is taken from the Cash Receipts Journal. The reference number is the page number of the Cash Receipts Journal. The amount received is listed under credit, and subtracted from the debit balance column. The debit balance column shows what the customer owes at all times.

Every record of a payment on the subsidiary ledger should be keyed to the invoices that have been paid. In Figure 6.11, for example, the payment of $231.50 was marked with an A. Since this payment was to cover invoice 1314, an A was also placed in front of that invoice amount in the debit column. The next time a payment is made, the letter B will be used to key off the matching invoices, then C, and so on. Sometimes payments may cover two or more invoices, in which case all of them would be keyed with the same letter.

TOPSY TOY CO.
100 Main St.
Orange, N.Y. 10000

Sales Rep: Marvin Jones

	date		reference #		① debit	② credit	③ debit balance	④
1	3	1	1314		(A) 231 35		231 35	
2	3	18	1342		506 -		737 35	
3	3	28	CM 1358			24 -	713 35	
4	4	3	C.R. 4			(A) 231 35	482 -	
5								
6								
7								
8								
9								
10								
11								
12								
13								
14								
15								

FIGURE 6.11. Subsidiary ledger sheet illustrating the posting of cash receipts.

DISCOUNTS

If you allow customers to take discounts for early payment of invoices, they should be recorded as follows: When you receive payment for an invoice, list the invoice amount, not the check amount, as a credit to Accounts Receivable. However, debit the difference to an account called "Discounts" in your General Ledger. You can itemize this under "General" or set up a separate column for it in your Cash Receipts Journal (see Figure 6.12).

If you want to keep track of individual discounts taken by your customers, add a "Discounts" column to your Subsidiary Ledger accounts and when posting payments from your Cash Receipts Journal, list discounts taken as illustrated in Figure 6.13.

When you are preparing financial statements, Discounts will be subtracted from Gross Sales in order to get a Net Sales figure. See Figure 11.18 in Chapter 11 for an example of this.

AGED TRIAL BALANCE

At the end of each month an aged trial balance should be prepared from the information on the subsidiary ledger. Figure 6.14 illustrates a typical trial balance for the month of June, 1996. The company illustrated allows 30-day payment terms to its customers. The "total due" is the debit balance figure from the subsidiary ledger (see the sample subsidiary ledger for this trial balance in Figure 6.15). The "current" figure includes all unpaid invoices billed during the month of June (in this case invoices 10533 and 10589). The 30-day figure includes all unpaid invoices billed in May (30 days past due). The 60-day figure includes all unpaid invoices billed in April. The 90-plus figure includes all unpaid invoices billed prior to April.

The total-due figure for all customers on your trial balance must agree with the total balance of your Accounts Receivable account in the General Ledger. If it doesn't, first recheck your footing (addition) of both figures. If your figures still do not match, you should go through your invoices for the month and check to be sure each one was entered in the Sales Journal or invoice tape and the debit column of the appropriate customer sheet in the subsidiary ledger. If you still can't find the error you should go through the Cash Receipts Journal and make sure that each Accounts Receivable entry was checked off (meaning it was listed on the subsidiary ledger).

One common error is to enter a credit memo as a regular invoice. All credit memos should be checked to be sure they have been listed properly as credits on subsidiary ledger sheets and subtracted from debit balances.

One way to track down an error is to see if the amount of the error matches

CASH RECEIPTS JOURNAL Page 6

	date	item	1 total	2 Accounts Receivable	3 Customer Discounts	4	5	6	
1	2-23	Topsy Toy Co.	226.72	231.35	(4.63)				1
2									2
3									3
4									4
5									5
6									6
7									7
8									8
9									9
10									10
11									11
12									12
13									13
14									14
15									15

FIGURE 6.12. Entry in the Cash Receipts Journal showing how to record payment for an invoice on which the customer has taken a discount. The check amount is listed under "total," the invoice amount under "accounts receivable," and the discount in the "general" column. Since this is a Cash Receipts Journal, the "total" column is debited to Cash. All other accounts are credited unless they are in parentheses, in which case they are debited. Since a discount taken by a customer is a debit, it is in parentheses in this example.

TOPSY TOY CO
100 Main St.
Orange, N.Y. 10000

Sales Rep: Marvin Jones

	date		reference #	① debit	② credit	③ discount	④ debit balance
1	3	1	1314	(A) 231 35			231 35
2	3	18	1342	506 –			737 35
3	3	28	CM 1358		24 –		713 35
4	4	3	CR-4		(A) 226 72	4 63	482 –
5							
6							
7							
8							
9							
10							
11							
12							
13							
14							
15							

FIGURE 6.13. List discounts taken by customers in a "discounts" column in a subsidiary ledger. Note that the $226.72 payment (A) and the discount of $4.63 equal the invoice amount (A) of $231.35.

a particular invoice or credit memo. If it doesn't, divide by two and see if *this* figure matches.

Once you've found and corrected any errors in your records, you can use the Aged Trial Balance as a tool in controlling past due accounts. See Chapter 7 on Credit and Collections for more information on how to do this.

SUMMING UP

In this chapter you learned how to maintain control over credit sales by issuing invoices and keeping copies of them in numerical order. You then keep track of monthly sales totals by taking an adding machine tape of that month's invoices; or by recording sales in a Sales Journal.

Monthly sales totals are then posted to the General Ledger by debiting Accounts Receivable and crediting Sales. Payments (from the Cash Receipts Journal) are posted as credits to Accounts Receivable and debits to Cash.

TRIAL BALANCE: June 30, 1996

	customer name	1 total due	2 current	3 30 days	4 60 days	5 90+days	6	
1	Aamco	6420	3210	2200	610	400		1
2	Colins Co.	520	520					2
3	Everett Inc.	3928	2678	1250				3
4	Fine & Fine	2010	1005	755	250			4
5	Lewis & Son	965	620	300	45			5
6	Lucky Leather	2845	1525	620	500	200		6
7	Madison Gift	897	897					7
8	Paper Prod. Co.	4500	3050	1450				8
9	Ronson Co.	2350	2150	150	50			9
10	Rubber Bubble	4000	1200	2050	750			10
11	Topsy Toy Co.	2405	1805	600				11
12		30840 -	18660 -	9375 -	2205 -	600 -		12
13								13
14								14
15								15
16								16
17								17
18								18
19								19
20								20

FIGURE 6.14. Aged trial balance. The first line figures are based on the subsidiary ledger in Figure 6.15.

AAMCO CORP.
800 50th St.
New York, N.Y. 10001

Sales Rep: Martin Spinner

	date		reference #		debit ①	credit ②	debit balance ③
1	2	28					2000
2	3	6	1034		(6)1500		3500
3	3	8	CR-5			(F)2000	1500
4	3	27	10362		400		1900
5	4	5	10401		610		2510
6	5	2	10435		1400		3910
7	5	15	10472		800		4710
8	5	20	CR-8			(6)1500	3210
9	6	7	10533		2100		5310
10	6	28	10589		1110		6420
11							
12							
13							
14							
15							

FIGURE 6.15. Sample subsidiary ledger illustrating the origin of the figures for the first line of the aged trial balance in Figure 6.14.

Subsidiary ledgers are useful for keeping track of individual customer accounts, and taking a monthly aged trial balance will provide information to help you maintain control over past due accounts.

7

Credit and Collections

Your systems for granting credit and handling collections are two sides of the same coin. The more care you take in granting credit in the first place, the less headaches you will have on the collection end.

A home heating oil company, for example, found that it didn't pay to give credit to people *renting* homes. Since many more of these people became delinquent than did home owners, the company made a policy not to grant credit to renters. The company may have lost some accounts because of this policy, but they felt their operation was more profitable in the long run.

You may be tempted to grant credit freely in order to increase sales, but this approach is extremely dangerous. No matter how well you run the rest of your business, poor credit policies can kill you. A customer who doesn't pay you is worthless. Take on too many of these accounts, and you'll quickly be swimming in red ink.

CREDIT POLICIES

The first thing to question is whether you should give credit at all. If you get cash up front in every transaction, you won't have to worry about delinquent accounts. If your business can remain competitive *without* offering credit, this is the simplest and safest way to operate.

Of course, even then you'll be faced with the problems associated with bad checks (unless you take cash only). To minimize the bad check problem, follow these guidelines:

1. Don't accept second party checks.
2. Accept no out-of-town checks.
3. Require at least two forms of identification, such as a driver's license and a major credit card.

IF YOU DECIDE TO OFFER CREDIT

For most businesses, it's necessary to allow customers to buy on credit. The key to success here is to be *selective*, in order to eliminate as many of the bad credit risks as possible.

The specific procedures you use to do this will depend on the type of business you're in, the average dollar amount of a typical sale, and the total dollar business you expect to do with a customer for the duration of your relationship.

Design your credit policies to cover the following:

1. *Who you will give credit to*. (If your customers are businesses, for example, the criteria you use might include: must be in business for three years, must have annual sales of $500,000 or more, must have three supplier references, etc.)
2. *How much credit you will give*. (For example, you might start out with a $500 credit limit for new customers, gradually increasing this amount if the customer pays promptly and regularly.)

Once you've set up your credit guidelines, you shouldn't waver from them without a *very good reason*. Periodically, of course, you should review your guidelines to see if they still fit your needs. If your guidelines are too strict, you may lose some good business. If they are too loose, you'll end up with too many bad risks. If you have to err, it's better to be on the conservative side.

TOOLS FOR CHECKING AN APPLICANT'S CREDIT WORTHINESS

Here are some of the tools you might find helpful in ascertaining whether or not a prospective customer meets your credit criteria:

1. Reports from a credit bureau
2. Bank references
3. References from other suppliers
4. The customer's financial statements

If you decide to use reports from a credit bureau, be sure to pick a bureau which will have accurate and useful information on *your* type of customers. Very often credit bureaus specialize in particular industries. Some handle individual consumers better than businesses, for example.

Also make sure the information you get is *accurate* and *up-to-date*. Check with other businesses in your industry to find out what credit sources *they* use, and why.

When you check with a credit applicant's references, try to speak to them in person or on the phone. Sometimes people will *tell* you things they will not put in writing. And keep in mind that the same customer may pay some suppliers in a timely fashion and keep others waiting.

Past history and healthy bank balances may indicate that a customer is a good risk. But another consideration is the clout *you* have. How important are your services to this customer? If it comes to a crunch, will you be one of the suppliers paid on time?

This lack of clout is one problem small businesses face in collections, especially when dealing with big businesses. You know the big business is good for the money, but you can't get them to pay you on time. Especially in times of high interest rates, they're likely to use *your* money to help *their* cash flow rather than borrowing money to pay you on time.

RECORDKEEPING AND REPORTS

Once you've established your credit policy covering who will be allowed credit, for what reasons, and for how much, the next step is to set up procedures for monitoring results.

First, you should make sure every customer will be billed in a timely and accurate manner, for every transaction. Delays in sending out invoices cost you money. Mistakes on invoices and statements irritate customers and delay payments. (See Chapter 6 for details on invoicing customers and keeping track of credit sales.)

Keeping track of payments, discounts, cancellations, and returns is also very important. You should have a system for flagging late payments, especially for large dollar amounts, so you can take action immediately.

Chapter 6 shows you how to take an aged trial balance so you can see which accounts are current and which are past due. By analyzing this information you can see how quickly money is coming in, and whether you need to do something to speed it up.

There are two things you should look for when analyzing your aged trial balance. First, you should look at *individual* accounts which are past due. Note any changes in payment patterns. If a good payer begins to get slower and slower, there may be a problem. Don't let the problem get too big before you do something about it.

The second thing to look for is the *overall* payment patterns of your customers. During recessions, for example, you may find it takes longer, on the average, to collect your money. You'll need to take this fact into consideration when making cash flow projections (see Chapter 15). Such a slowdown may also signal a need for tighter than normal credit policies. For example, you may need to have stricter criteria in granting credit during such times.

COLLECTING DELINQUENT ACCOUNTS

There are many ways to handle delinquent accounts. Some companies automatically send a statement or a copy of the invoice marked "past due" when a payment is a specified number of days late. Such routine reminders at least bring the bill again to the customer's attention.

But for some accounts this won't be enough. You need something more forceful once a bill has reached a later stage of delinquency. Letters, phone calls, and eventually even legal action may be called for.

There are several things to consider when planning a procedure for collecting delinquent accounts:

1. How much time and money can you afford to invest in the collection process?
2. Are you planning to continue the relationship with the delinquent customer after the collection?
3. What kind of leverage do you have? For example, can you cut off delivery of a needed commodity? Are you the customer's sole supplier, or can they go elsewhere?
4. What is likely to be the most *effective* method of collection you can afford?

It will probably take some experimenting to find the best method for your company. This is another reason it's important to keep careful records. If you try two different collection agencies, for example, you'll need to keep good records to know which one was more successful.

Many companies find the telephone more effective than letters. Usually some combination of the two is used. One advantage of the telephone is that you can modify your remarks in accordance with the customer's responses.

The newsletter *Better Communication** offers the following approach to telephone persuasion:

> The best approach is to say very little. Let the debtor do the talking. For example:
>
> Debtor: "Joyce Franklin."
>
> You: "Joyce, this is Bob Jones from Al Corporation. I'm calling about your past due bill with us for $240.00."
>
> At this point, you should keep quiet and listen to what Joyce has to say. Unless

---

* *Better Communication* is published by INFORMATION PLUS, 175 Washington Valley Rd., Warren, N.J. 07060

she is a deadbeat, or she denies the validity of your claim, she will make apologies and promise to send a check.

Before getting off the phone, you should get a firm commitment as to when she will send a check, and for how much. If she tries to put it off, ask her to send at least part of it immediately. And let her know that you will be personally looking for her check.

In collection letters, it's very important not to threaten or insult your customer. Be firm and straightforward, but don't be rude.

Here's an example of a collection letter, also from *Better Communication:*

Dear Mr. Doe:

In reviewing our files we find that you have an outstanding balance of $73.19.

No payments have been made on your account since this charge was made on January 3, three months ago.

May we have your check for this amount, a payment on account, or some explanation for non-payment?

Sincerely yours,

Bob's Seafood House

Whatever you try to do to collect your money, be careful not to do anything illegal. If you telephone a debtor too often, too late at night, or too early in the morning, for example, you might be sued for harrassment.

In letters, don't make any threats you really don't plan to carry out. For example, if you say you will turn the account over to a lawyer or a collection agency if it's not paid, you'd better do it. You mustn't misrepresent the legal status of your claim or make idle threats.

When All Else Fails. If you can't collect your money through phone calls and letters, you have three other options:

1. *Legal suit.* If you're a local business, consider taking debtors to small claims court. For large amounts or out-of-town claims, however, you'll need a lawyer, and this can be expensive.
2. *Collection agencies.* Before simply writing off the debt as uncollectible, you might try giving it to an agency. Most agencies work on a percentage basis, charging from 10% to 50%, depending on the amount of the debt and what they have to do to collect it.

3. *Writing off the debt as uncollectible.* Bad debts are a legitimate business expense. But the IRS wants to be sure you've made every effort to collect the debt first, especially if it's a sizeable one. If the IRS should question your bad debt expense, you'll have to document to the agent's satisfaction that you made every reasonable effort to collect, but could not. You should therefore save correspondence with customers, collection agencies, and attorneys. Keep a record of notes on phone calls made to customers regarding old accounts.

ACCOUNTING FOR BAD DEBTS

There are two methods of accounting for bad debts that are acceptable to the Internal Revenue Service for tax purposes: (1) the direct write-off method; and (2) the reserve method.

The Direct Write-Off Method. This is the simplest method. Under this method you increase bad debt expense when you determine that an individual account cannot be collected; that is, when your last collection effort has failed.

Simply make a journal entry to debit Bad Debt Expense and credit Accounts Receivable for the amount of the invoice or invoices you want to write off. Also make an entry in those customers' accounts in the Accounts Receivable Subsidiary Ledger (see Chapter 6), if you have one, to remove the receivables from their balance.

If a customer (whose balance you have written off) later pays you, you'll reduce bad debt expense for the amount paid. In the journal entry, debit Cash and credit Bad Debt Expense.

The Reserve Method. Under this method you set up a reserve for bad debts, which is an offset to Accounts Receivable. The reserve is an estimate of the amount in Accounts Receivable which is not collectible. Since IRS rules for using the reserve method are quite complex, we won't describe it fully here, but suggest you consult your accountant or tax specialist.

ACCOUNTING FOR COLLECTION FEES

You can pay collection fees to agencies and lawyers in two ways: (1) they may deduct their fees directly from monies collected, sending you the balance; or (2) they may send you all the monies collected and then bill you for their services. The recordkeeping for each of these is slightly different.

If you get a bill for services, the amount will be recorded in your Cash

Disbursements Journal when you pay it. You can either have a separate column for Collection Fees or put them under the General column. When these fees are posted to the General Ledger, they will be debited to Collection Fees Expense and credited to Cash.

If the fees are deducted from the monies collected, you would record the transaction in your Cash Receipts Journal. For example, suppose your collection agency collected a debt of $150 and kept $30 as a collection fee, sending you the $120. The General Ledger entry for this transaction would be as follows:

Debit: Cash $120.00

Credit: Accounts Receivable $150.00. (You must reduce the total amount of the Accounts Receivable from the Accounts Receivable balance because it is no longer owed to you. If you have an Accounts Receivable subsidiary ledger, the full amount should be deducted from your customer's balance here, also.)

Debit: Collection Fees Expense $30.00.

SUMMING UP

In any business, collecting monies owed is just as important as making sales. Without the proper control over credit extension and delinquent account collection, these areas of a business can easily get out of hand and cause serious cash flow problems at best—and at worst, actual business losses.

Accurate recordkeeping and timely reports can help you to maintain control over this critical end of your business. By establishing sound credit extension policies and monitoring carefully the timeliness of payments, you should be able to minimize your collection efforts and maintain a healthy cash flow.

8

Accounting For Fixed Assets

This chapter will give you a general understanding of how to account for fixed assets. The concepts behind fixed assets accounting are simple. The tax legislation affecting fixed assets, however, is extremely complex and frequently changed. This chapter won't prepare you to determine depreciation expense for income tax purposes, or even to decide which expenditures should be capitalized and which should be expensed for tax purposes. The advice of your accountant or tax specialist is critical in this area.

THE NATURE OF FIXED ASSETS

Fixed assets, also commonly referred to as "Property, Plant and Equipment", are long-lived assets used in your business. The costs of these assets are "capitalized"; that is, recorded as assets on the business balance sheet, and depreciated, or expensed, over the assets' useful lives.

The categories of fixed assets your business might own include:

Land. Land should be recorded on your balance sheet at the amount you paid for it. Land is the only fixed asset that shouldn't be depreciated, since its value can't be used up or depreciated.

Buildings. This would include the amounts spent to purchase or construct buildings used in your business.

Improvements. This includes the costs of alterations or improvements to buildings owned or leased. If you lease your business facilities, you would call the improvements you make "leasehold improvements". Only major betterments should be included, not ongoing repairs.

Furniture and fixtures. Includes the cost of any furniture and fixtures such as lighting and shelves, and carpeting.

Equipment. Includes all office, factory and store equipment.

Vehicles. Cars, trucks and tractors used in your business.

CAPITALIZE VS. EXPENSE

Whether you should capitalize an expenditure and depreciate it over some period of time, or immediately expense it, will depend on two factors: (1) the useful life of the asset purchased, and (2) the dollar amount of the expenditure.

Useful Life. You should only capitalize assets that have useful lives of more than two years. Generally, there is no point in capitalizing items that must be replaced every year or two. You will only create a lot of unnecessary bookkeeping work.

Dollar amount of expenditure. You should set a minimum dollar amount for expenditures that you will capitalize. If you capitalize $25 expenditures because the asset will last several years, you'll spend all your time in recordkeeping and have no time to run your business. A minimum of $100, $200 or even $500 or more may be reasonable, depending on the nature and size of your business. This is something you should discuss with your accountant.

RECORDING FIXED ASSET PURCHASES

When you purchase fixed assets, make an entry in your Cash Disbursements Journal as shown in Figure 8.1. This entry will be posted to the debit side of a Fixed Assets account in your General Ledger (see Figure 8.2).

The purchase of fixed assets should also be recorded in a schedule as illustrated in Figure 8.3. A separate schedule should be prepared for each year's acquisitions. Note that there is a place to list the cost of the asset, its estimated useful life, the depreciation method you are using (see below), and the amount of depreciation taken each year. Every time you purchase a fixed asset, add it to this schedule. When you compute depreciation at the end of the year, list it in the applicable column for that year. The fixed asset purchases on this schedule should agree with the acquisitions in your Fixed Asset account in the General Ledger.

DEPRECIATION METHODS

Depreciation is the process of estimating and recording lost usefulness of fixed assets. It can also be viewed as a way to spread the cost of an asset over its useful life.

There are various methods that can be used to calculate depreciation for accounting purposes. These methods can also be used for income tax purposes to depreciate assets purchased before January 1, 1981.

CASH DISBURSEMENTS JOURNAL Page 2

	date	payee	check #	total	Accounts Payable	Salaries	Supplies	General Amount	General Account			
			1	2	3	4	5	6	7	8	9	10
1	2-14	Mahwah Oldsmobile	1278	10000-				10000-	Vehicles			
2												
3												
4												
5												
6												
7												
8												
9												
10												

FIGURE 8.1. Cash Disbursements Journal showing the entry of a fixed asset purchase.

VEHICLES

date	items	folio	debits	date	items	folio	credits
2-14		CD-2	10000 -				

FIGURE 8.2. The fixed asset purchase recorded in the Cash Disbursements Journal in Figure 8.1 posted to the debit side of the Fixed Assets General Ledger account.

FIXED ASSET PURCHASES - 1996

Date	Vendor	Cost	Estimated Usefull Life	Salvage Value and Dep. Meth.	1st YR	2nd YR	3rd YR	4th YR	5th YR	6th YR	7th YR
	Machinery + Equipment										
2-14	Allied Mach. Corp.	10 000-	10 yrs.	db-20%							
3-17	Hunter Equip Co.	3000-	5 yrs.	db-15%							
	VEHICLES										
1-9	Mahwah Oldsmobile	10000-	4 yrs	S.L.-2,000-							

FIGURE 8.3. How to set up a Fixed Assets Purchases Schedule.

The Accelerated Cost Recovery System (ACRS) which is part of the Economic Recovery Tax Act of 1981, radically altered depreciation rules for assets purchased in 1981 and thereafter. The complexity of ACRS puts it beyond the scope of this book.

The following depreciation methods can be used for accounting purposes, and for tax purposes for assets purchased before January 1, 1981.

Straight Line. Straight line depreciation is calculated as follows:

$$\frac{\text{Cost less salvage value}}{\text{estimated useful life}} = \text{annual depreciation}$$

EXAMPLE. You purchase a $10,000 machine with an estimated useful life of 10 years. You also estimate that you will be able to sell the machine at the end of the 10 years for $500. Your annual depreciation expense would be $950:

$$\frac{10{,}000 - 500}{10} = \frac{9500}{10} = 950$$

Declining-Balance Method. This is known as an accelerated depreciation method, since it allows you to charge higher depreciation expense in the first years after purchase of a fixed asset, and lower amounts in later years. By using the declining-balance method, your income taxes will be lower during the first years after purchase and higher in later years.

For *new* equipment with minimum useful life of three years:

Year 1:	Take a percentage double the straight-line method
Each remaining year:	Take same percentage of remainder (book value)

EXAMPLE. A new machine with a useful life of 10 years is purchased for $10,000. It would be depreciated at 10 percent per year using straight line (see above). Under declining balance, you would use double, or 20 percent.

Year 1: 20 percent of $10,000 = $2,000
Year 2: 20 percent of $8,000 ($10,000 – $2,000) = $1,600
Year 3: 20 percent of $6,400 ($8,000 – $1,600) = $1,280
Year 4: 20 percent of $5,120 ($6,400 – $1,280) = $1,024
And so on

For *used* equipment with minimum useful life of three years:

Year 1:	Take a percentage 1½ times the straight-line method
Each remaining year:	Take same percentage of book value (cost less depreciation to date)

EXAMPLE. A used machine with a useful life of 10 years is purchased for $10,000. It would be depreciated at 10 percent per year using straight line. Under declining balance, you would use 1½ times, or 15 percent.

Year 1: 15 percent of $10,000 = $1,500
Year 2: 15 percent of $8,500 ($10,000 - $1,500) = $1,275
Year 3: 15 percent of $7,225 ($8,500 - $1,275) = $1,083.75
And so on

The salvage value of fixed assets is not considered under the declining-balance method, except that you may not depreciate an asset beyond its estimated salvage value.

Sum of the Year's Digits Method. This is another accelerated depreciation method. Under this method, the asset cost, less the estimated salvage value, is multiplied by a fraction. The denominator (bottom number) of the fraction is the sum of the year's digits. To find the sum of the year's digits, the digits of each year of the asset's life are progressively numbered and then added up. The numerator (top number) of the fraction is the digit of the highest year for year 1, then the second highest for year 2, etc.

EXAMPLE. A machine with a useful life of 4 years is purchased for $5,500. Estimated salvage value is $500. The depreciable base (cost less salvage value) is therefore $5,000.

The sum of the year's digits for four years is:

$$4 + 3 + 2 + 1 = 10$$

Depreciation expense will be:

1st year	=	4/10 of 5,000	=	2,000
2nd year	=	3/10 of 5,000	=	1,500
3rd year	=	2/10 of 5,000	=	1,000
4th year	=	1/10 of 5,000	=	500
Total depreciation			=	5,000

RECORDING DEPRECIATION EXPENSE

Depreciation expense should be entered on your schedule of fixed assets as shown in Figure 8.4. Note that assets purchased during the year are

FIXED ASSET PURCHASES - 1996

Date	Vendor	Cost	Estimated Useful Life	Dep. Method & Salvage Value	1st YR	2nd YR	3rd YR	4th YR	5th YR	6th YR	7th YR
	Machinery & Equipment										
1-3	Allied Mach. Co.	10000 -	10 YRS.	db-20%	2000 -						
6-2	Hunter Equip Co.	3000 -	5 YRS.	SL-300 -	270						
	Vehicles										
1-9	Mahwah Oldsmobile	10000 -	4 yrs.	SL-2000 -	2000 -						

FIGURE 8.4. First-year depreciation computed and entered in Fixed Assets Purchases schedule. In the first entry the declining balance method was used. The 20 percent (double the straight line of one-tenth or 10 percent) of \$10,000 is \$2,000. In the second entry, the straight-line method was used and the machine has a salvage value of \$300. The 20 percent (one-fifth) of \$2,700 is \$540. Since the machine was purchased in June, only one-half year's depreciation can be taken the first year ($\frac{1}{2} \times \$540 = \$270$). In the third entry, the straight-line method was used and the vehicle has a salvage value of \$2,000 ($\frac{1}{4} \times \$8,000 = \$2,000$).

depreciated at an appropriate fraction for the first year, that is, if you bought the asset in June, you would depreciate it for six months, or half the normal amount. To avoid having to compute depreciation for odd fractions of a year, you can use an average, charging one-half year's depreciation at the end of the year for all assets purchased within that year, no matter in what month they were purchased.

Next, make an entry in your General Journal as shown in Figure 8.5. The depreciation is then posted in the General Ledger as a debit to Depreciation Expense and a credit to Accumulated Depreciation (see Figure 8.6). The total depreciation expense for the year will appear on your income statement as illustrated in Figure 8.7. The total accumulated depreciation will be listed on your balance sheet under Fixed Assets as shown in Figure 8.8.

After your financial statements are prepared, the Depreciation Expense account will be cleared for the next year, as are all income and expense accounts. However, the Fixed Assets and Accumulated Depreciation accounts will continue to increase as equipment is purchased and depreciation is taken in the future. The balance in the Fixed Asset account will always be the total cost of equipment on hand. The balance in the Accumulated Depreciation account will always be the total depreciation taken on the assets in the Fixed

GENERAL JOURNAL Page 3

	date	description	debit	credit
1	12-31	Depreciation Expense	4270 -	
2		Accumulated Depreciation		4270 -
3		1996 Depreciation		
4				
5				
6				
7				
8				
9				
10				
11				
12				
13				
14				
15				
16				
17				
18				
19				
20				
21				

FIGURE 8.5. Depreciation recorded in the General Journal.

DEPRECIATION EXPENSE

date	items	folio	debits	date	items	folio	credits
12-31		GJ-3	4270 -				

ACCUMULATED DEPRECIATION

date	items	folio	debits	date	items	folio	credits
				12-31		GJ-3	4270 -

FIGURE 8.6. Posting of depreciation as a debit to Depreciation Expense and a credit to Accumulated Depreciation.

Assets account. Only when you sell or scrap the asset will it be written off in these two accounts. We see how this is done below.

INCOME STATEMENT FROM 1/1/96 TO 12/31/96

Sales		$100,000
Operating Expenses		
Rent	10,000	
Salaries	40,000	
Supplies	5,000	
Insurance	1,000	
Promotion	10,000	
Depreciation Expense	4,270*	
Utilities	1,000	
Miscellaneous	5,000	
Total Operating Expenses		76,270
Income		$ 23,730
Retained Earnings, Beginning Year:		5,000
Retained Earnings, End of Year:		$ 28,730

* This is the total depreciation expense for the year

FIGURE 8.7. Income Statement showing Depreciation Expense listed as an operating expense.

Selling a Fixed Asset at Net Book Value. Suppose you sell a machine that cost you $10,000 for $500 after having charged a total depreciation of $9,500 over the 10-year period. You would list the $500 in your Cash Receipts Journal and it would be posted as a debit to Cash and a Credit to Fixed Assets.

You no longer have the machine, however, so you would enter the $9,500 in your General Journal as a debit to Accumulated Depreciation and a credit to Fixed Assets. When this entry is posted to the Accumulated Depreciation and Fixed Assets accounts, the new balances will reflect a deduction of the $9,500 machine. This means it will no longer appear on your balance sheet as part of Fixed Assets or Accumulated Depreciation. Here's a summary of the procedure:

(a) Machine is purchased.
(b) 10 years of depreciation on straight-line method: 10 × $950 = $9,500.
(c) Machine is sold at net book value (original cost less accumulated depreciation = $500).
(d) Machine is written off books.

BALANCE SHEET AS OF 12/31/96

Current Assets			*Liabilities*		
Cash		$20,000	Loans Payable		$ 3,500
Prepaid Supplies		1,000	*Owner's Equity*		
Prepaid Insurance		500	Owner's Capital account	4,000	
		21,500	Retained Earnings	28,730	
Fixed Assets					32,730
Machinery & Equipment	13,000				
Vehicles	6,000				
	19,000				
Less Accumulated Depreciation	4,270*				
		14,730			
Total Assets		$36,230	*Total Liabilities & Owner's Equity*		$36,230

* Since this is the first year of operation for this company, Accumulated Depreciation is the same amount as the Depreciation Expense shown on the Income Statement in Figure 8.7. In future years the Accumulated Depreciation will include prior years' Depreciation Expense.

FIGURE 8.8. Balance Sheet showing how Accumulated Depreciation is subtracted from fixed assets.

Cash

debit (+)	credit (−)
500 (c)	10,000 (a)

Fixed Assets

debit (+)	credit (−)
10,000 (a)	500 (c)
	9,500 (d)
	balance = 0

Depreciation Expense

debit (+)	credit (−)
9,500 (b)	
	$9,500 of depreciation charged over 10-year period

Accumulated Depreciation

debit (−)	credit (+)
9,500 (d)	9,500 (b)
	balance = 0

Selling a Fixed Asset Before It's Fully Depreciated. As stated above, the book value of an asset is what's left after accumulated depreciation is subtracted from the original cost. A $10,000 machine that is depreciated $950 the first year will have a book value of $9,050. After a second year's depreciation it will have a book value of $8,100, and so forth. You may sell or scrap a fixed asset during its useful life either for more or less than its book value at that time. Examples are given below to show you how to record such a transaction (1) when you sell the asset at less than the book value, and (2) when you sell it for more than the book value.

EXAMPLE 1. A $10,000 machine is purchased. Estimated useful life is 10 years. Estimated salvage value is $500. Depreciation method is straight line. At the beginning of the tenth year, the machine is sold for $700. At that time $8,550 has been charged off in depreciation expense, leaving a book value of $1,450 ($10,000 minus $8,550).

(a) Machine is purchased.
(b) Nine years of accumulated depreciation (9 × $950 = $8,550).
(c) Machine is sold for $700.
(d) Loss on sale of asset is charged (book value minus sale price is $1450 − $700 = $750).
(e) Machine is written off as an asset.

Cash

debit (+)	credit (−)
700 (c)	10,000 (a)

Fixed Assets

debit (+)	credit (−)
10,000 (a)	1,450 (c) + (d) 8,550 (e)
	balance = 0

Depreciation Expense

debit (+)	credit (−)
8,550 (b)	
	$8,550 of depreciation charged over a 9-year period

Accumulated Depreciation

debit (−)	credit (+)
8,550 (e)	8,550 (b)
	balance = 0

Loss on Sale of Assets

debit (+)	credit (−)
750 (d)	
	balance = $750 debit

EXAMPLE 2. A $10,000 machine is purchased. Estimated useful life is 10 years. Estimated salvage value is $500. Depreciation method is straight line. At the beginning of the tenth year, the machine is sold for $1,500. At that time $8,550 has been charged off to depreciation expense, leaving a book value of $1,450 ($10,000 minus $8,550).

(a) Machine is purchased.
(b) Nine years of accumulated depreciation (9 × $950 = $8,550).
(c) Machine is sold for $1,500. Book value of $1,450 is $50 less than sale price of $1,500, so profit of $50 was made.
(d) Machine is written off as an asset.

Cash

debit (+)	credit (−)
1,500 (c)	10,000 (a)

Fixed Assets

debit (+)	credit (−)
10,000 (a)	1,450 (c)
	8,550 (d)
	balance = 0

Depreciation Expense

debit (+)	credit (−)
8,550 (b)	
	$8,550 depreciation expense charged over a 9-year period

Accumulated Depreciation

debit (−)	credit (+)
8,550 (d)	8,550 (b)
	balance = 0

Gain on Sale of Assets

debit (−)	credit (+)
	50 (c)
	balance = $50 credit

SUMMING UP

The original cost of fixed assets and the accumulated depreciation should be listed on your balance sheet. Land will remain on the balance sheet at its original cost, since land cannot be depreciated.

The depreciation methods described in this chapter may not be appropriate for income tax purposes. Consult with your accountant or tax specialist before recording depreciation expense.

9

Payroll

When you hire employees to work in your business, you automatically become subject to various city, state, and federal laws requiring you to withhold income and social security taxes from wages; pay employer's share of social security and unemployment taxes; and provide your employees with worker's compensation and disability insurance.

The first step in becoming an employer is to register with city (if your city has withholding taxes), state, and federal governments. Figure 9.1 shows a federal employer registration form. You'll be assigned an identification number which will be used when paying taxes and filing forms. You'll also receive an *Employer's Tax Guide* from the Internal Revenue Service and a similar employer's handbook from your state and city governments. You should read these guides carefully to make sure you are complying fully with the applicable withholding, payment, and filing requirements.

HIRING AN EMPLOYEE

When you hire employees, have them fill out a W-4 form (Figure 9.2) on or before their first day of work. You must know their social security number, total exemptions claimed, and marital status in order to compute their payroll taxes. Employees who are exempt from withholding taxes must fill out Form W-4E if they don't want taxes withheld from their pay. Employees should also fill out a city or state withholding exemption certificate or both, if applicable (see Figure 9.3).

PREPARING PAYROLL

A payroll book as illustrated in Figure 9.4 is handy for recording employee hours worked, wages, and deductions. "Fed. O.A.T." stands for Federal Old Age Tax, also known as FOAT, social security taxes, or, most commonly FICA. The employer's tax guide contains a FICA tax table to save you the trouble of computing it.

☆ U. S. GOVERNMENT PRINTING OFFICE: 1974 — 535-411

Δ

FOR CLEAR COPY ON ALL PARTS TYPEWRITE OR PRINT WITH BALL POINT PEN—PRESS FIRMLY
(See Instructions on Reverse)

FORM SS-4 (3-69)
PART 1 U.S. TREASURY DEPARTMENT—INTERNAL REVENUE SERVICE
APPLICATION FOR EMPLOYER IDENTIFICATION NUMBER

1. NAME *(TRUE name as distinguished from TRADE name.)*

2. TRADE NAME, IF ANY *(Enter name under which business is operated, if different from item 1.)*

3. ADDRESS OF PRINCIPAL PLACE OF BUSINESS *(No. and Street, City, State, Zip Code)* | 4. COUNTY OF BUSINESS LOCATION

5. ORGANIZATION Check Type ☐ Individual ☐ Partnership ☐ Corporation ☐ Other *(specify e.g. estate, trust, etc.)* ☐ Governmental (See Instr. 5) ☐ Nonprofit Organization (See Instr. 5) | 6. Ending Month of Accounting year

7. REASON FOR APPLYING *(If "other" specify such as "Corporate structure change," "Acquired by gift or trust," etc.)* ☐ Started new business ☐ Purchased going business ☐ Other | 8. Date you acquired or started business *(Mo., day, year)* | 9. First date you paid or will pay wages *(Mo., day, year)*

10. NATURE OF BUSINESS *(See Instructions)* | 11. NUMBER OF EMPLOYEES→ IF "NONE" ENTER "0" | Non-agricultural | Agricultural

12. If nature of business is MANUFACTURING, list in order of their importance the principal products manufactured and the estimated percentage of the total value of all products which each represents. A % B % C %

PLEASE LEAVE BLANK: R | DO | TA | FR | FRC

13. Do you operate more than one place of business? ☐ Yes ☐ No
If "Yes, attach a list showing for each separate establishment: a. Name and address. b. Nature of business c. Number of employees.

14. To whom do you sell most of your products or services? ☐ Business establishments ☐ General public ☐ Other *(Specify)*

PLEASE LEAVE BLANK → Geo. | Ind. | Class | Size | Reas. for Appl. | Bus. Bir. Date

FORM SS-4 (3-69)
PART 2 DO NOT DETACH ANY PART OF THIS FORM. SEND ALL COPIES TO
INTERNAL REVENUE SERVICE

PLEASE LEAVE BLANK

NAME AND COMPLETE ADDRESS

1. NAME *(TRUE name as distinguished from TRADE name.)*

2. TRADE NAME, IF ANY *(Enter name under which business is operated, if different from item 1.)*

3. ADDRESS OF PRINCIPAL PLACE OF BUSINESS *(No. and Street)*

(City, State, Zip Code) | 4. COUNTY OF BUSINESS LOCATION

5. ORGANIZATION Check Type ☐ Individual ☐ Partnership ☐ Corporation ☐ Other *(specify e.g. estate, trust, etc.)* ☐ Governmental (See Instr. 5) ☐ Nonprofit Organization (See Instr. 5) | 6. Ending Month of Accounting year

7. REASON FOR APPLYING *(If "other" specify such as "Corporate structure change," "Acquired by gift or trust," etc.)* ☐ Started new business ☐ Purchased going business ☐ Other | 8. Date you acquired or started business *(Mo., day, year)* | 9. First date you paid or will pay wages *(Mo., day, year)*

10. NATURE OF BUSINESS *(See Instructions)* | 11. NUMBER OF EMPLOYEES→ IF "NONE" ENTER "0" | Non-agricultural | Agricultural

12. Have you ever applied for an identification number for this or any other business? ☐ No ☐ Yes
If "Yes," enter name and trade name (if any). Also enter the approximate date, city, and state where you first applied and previous number if known. →

DATE | SIGNATURE | TITLE

FIGURE 9.1. Application for employer identification number from the United States Treasury Department.

Form **W-4** (Rev January 1982) — Department of the Treasury—Internal Revenue Service — **Employee's Withholding Allowance Certificate** — OMB No. 1545-0010 Expires 4-30-83

1 Type or print your full name	2 Your social security number
Home address (number and street or rural route)	3 Marital Status: ☐ Single ☐ Married ☐ Married, but withhold at higher Single rate
City or town, State, and ZIP code	**Note:** If married, but legally separated, or spouse is a nonresident alien, check the Single box.

4 Total number of allowances you are claiming (from line F of the worksheet on page 2) . . . .

5 Additional amount, if any, you want deducted from each pay . . . . $

6 I claim exemption from withholding because (see instructions and check boxes below that apply):

a ☐ Last year I did not owe any Federal income tax and had a right to a full refund of **ALL** income tax withheld, **AND**

b ☐ This year I do not expect to owe any Federal income tax and expect to have a right to a full refund of **ALL** income tax withheld. If both a and b apply, enter "EXEMPT" here . . . . ▶

c If you entered "EXEMPT" on line 6b, are you a full-time student? . . . . ☐ **Yes** ☐ **No**

Under the penalties of perjury, I certify that I am entitled to the number of withholding allowances claimed on this certificate, or if claiming exemption from withholding, that I am entitled to claim the exempt status.

Employee's signature ▶ Date ▶ , 19

7 Employer's name and address (including ZIP code) (FOR EMPLOYER'S USE ONLY)	8 Office code	9 Employer identification number

FIGURE 9.2. W-4 form which must be filled out by employees on or before their first day of work.

Federal withholding tax is based on the marital status and number of exemptions an employee claims. Again, tables are provided in the employer's tax guide. Your state and city guides also provide tables for computing state and city withholding taxes.

If you have pension or other insurance programs to which the employee contributes, there is space to list these deductions in your payroll book. You then add up the deductions and compute the net pay for each employee.

When you pay your employees, you can write a check for the net amount and give the employee a statement itemizing deductions, as illustrated in Figure 9.5. Or you may wish to keep a separate payroll account at your bank,

IT-2104 (1/72)
State of New York
Dept. of Taxation and Finance

NEW YORK STATE - EMPLOYEE'S WITHHOLDING EXEMPTION CERTIFICATE

Print full name .... Social Security No. ....

Print home address .... City .... State .... ZIP Code ....

EMPLOYEE: File this exemption certificate with your employer if you choose to claim New York State withholding tax exemptions different from those used for Federal withholding purposes.

EMPLOYER: Keep exemption certificates with your records. Certificates may be on this form, or a similar form. If the employee is believed to have claimed too many exemptions, notify the Director, Income Tax Bureau.

HOW TO CLAIM YOUR WITHHOLDING EXEMPTIONS

1. Personal exemption for yourself. Write "1" if claimed . . . .
2. If married, personal exemption for your wife (or husband) if not separately claimed by her(him). Write "1" if claimed . . . .
3. Special withholding allowance if claimed on Federal Form W-4. Write "1" if claimed. ....
4. Exemptions for age and blindness (applicable only to you and your wife but not to dependents):
   (a) If you or your wife will be 65 years of age or older at the end of the year, and you claim this exemption, write the figure "1"; if both will be 65 or older, and you claim both of these exemptions, write the figure "2" . . . .
   (b) If you or your wife are blind, and you claim this exemption, write the figure "1"; if both are blind, and you claim both of these exemptions, write the figure "2" . . . .
5. Exemptions for dependents. Write the number of such exemptions claimed . . . .
6. Withholding allowances for itemized deductions claimed on Federal Form W-4 (See instructions on other side) . . . .
7. Add the number of exemptions and allowances claimed above and write the total . . . . ☐
8. Additional withholding per pay period under agreement with employer . . . . $ ....

I CERTIFY that the number of withholding exemptions claimed on this certificate does not exceed the number to which I am entitled.

(Date) .... , 19 .... (Signed) ....

FIGURE 9.3. State withholding exemption certificate.

MUTUAL NO. SS-12 PAYROLL WEEK ENDING ________________ 19 ____

• NAME OF EMPLOYEE	• DAYS AND HOURS									• WAGES				• EMPLOYEE DEDUCTIONS							• NET AMOUNT PAYABLE
								TOTAL REG. TIME	TOTAL OVER TIME	WAGE RATE	REGULAR WAGES	OVRTIME WAGES	TOTAL WAGES	FED. O.A.T.	FED. WITH. TAX	STATE WITH. TAX	CITY WITH. TAX	SICKNESS DISBLTY		TOTAL DEDUCT.	
1																					
2																					
3																					
4																					
5																					
6																					
7																					
8																					
9																					

FIGURE 9.4. Page from a payroll book useful for recording employee hours worked, wages, and deductions.

STATEMENT OF EARNINGS

Name Smat Kirsner

Soc. Sec. No. 121-24-8820

Period From 1/2 19 95 To 1/6 19 95

Total Earnings $ 200.00

Deductions

FICA 11.70

FED WITHHOLDING TAX 24.10

STATE WITHHOLDING TAX 3.40

UNEMPLOYMENT INS ____

CREDIT UNION ____

TOTAL DEDUCTIONS 39.20

NET AMOUNT PAID 160.80

EMPLOYER Master Marketing

FIGURE 9.5. Itemized statement showing employees their gross pay, deductions, and net pay.

using specially designed payroll checks which come with a stub for itemization of deductions. In this case you would deposit enough money in your payroll checking account to cover your payroll each period. Ask your banker to describe your bank's payroll checking account plans.

PAYING PAYROLL TAXES

You may be required to pay the following payroll taxes:

City, state, and federal withholding, deducted from employees' pay.

Social security taxes (FICA), employees' share plus employer's share.

State and federal unemployment taxes, usually paid by employer.

Federal withholding and social security taxes will be paid in a combined payment monthly or quarterly, depending on the amount due (see your tax guide). If you make monthly deposits, you can use a Tax Deposit Form 501 (Figure 9.6), which will be provided you by the Internal Revenue Service. These deposits can be made to any qualified commerical bank or a Federal Reserve Bank (check with your bank to find out if they are a qualified depository).

Every employer must file quarterly returns (Form 941, as illustrated in Figure 9.7) for federal withholding and social security taxes. Any balance of payments due must be paid when filing this form.

Federal unemployment taxes are payable once a year with the filing of Form 940. You will be given partial credit on this form for contributions to any state unemployment tax fund.

State unemployment taxes may be payable quarterly or yearly, with the filing of an applicable form. Your state tax guide has this information.

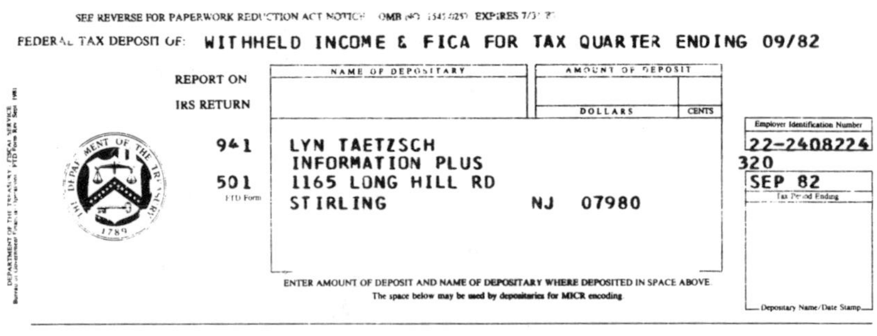
FEDERAL TAX DEPOSIT OF: WITHHELD INCOME & FICA FOR TAX QUARTER ENDING 09/82

REPORT ON IRS RETURN 941 501

NAME OF DEPOSITARY | AMOUNT OF DEPOSIT (DOLLARS, CENTS)

LYN TAETZSCH
INFORMATION PLUS
1165 LONG HILL RD
STIRLING NJ 07980

Employer Identification Number 22-2408224
320
SEP 82 Tax Period Ending

ENTER AMOUNT OF DEPOSIT AND NAME OF DEPOSITARY WHERE DEPOSITED IN SPACE ABOVE
The space below may be used by depositaries for MICR encoding

Depositary Name/Date Stamp

FIGURE 9.6. Tax Deposit Form 501 to be used when making monthly deposits of federal withholding and FICA taxes.

Form **941** (Rev. January 1982) Department of the Treasury Internal Revenue Service

Employer's Quarterly Federal Tax Return

▶ For Paperwork Reduction Act Notice, see page 2.

OMB No. 1545-0029
Expires 10-31-82

Your name, address, employer identification number, and calendar quarter of return. (If not correct, please change.) ▶

Name (as distinguished from trade name) | Date quarter ended

Trade name, if any | Employer identification number

Address and ZIP code

T
FF
FD
FP
I
T

If address is different from prior return, check here ▶ ☐

Record of Federal Tax Liability and Deposits

If you are a first-time 3-banking-day depositor (see Specific Instructions on page 4) check here . . . ▶ ☐

	a. Date wages paid	b. Tax liability	c. Date of deposit	d. Amount deposited
	Day	Overpayment from previous quarter . . ▶		
First month of quarter	1st–3rd A			
	4th–7th B			
	8th–11th C			
	12th–15th D			
	16th–19th E			
	20th–22nd F			
	23rd–25th G			
	26th–last H			
I	Total . . ▶			
Second month of quarter	1st–3rd I			
	4th–7th J			
	8th–11th K			
	12th–15th L			
	16th–19th M			
	20th–22nd N			
	23rd–25th O			
	26th–last P			
II	Total . . ▶			
Third month of quarter	1st–3rd Q			
	4th–7th R			
	8th–11th S			
	12th–15th T			
	16th–19th U			
	20th–22nd V			
	23rd–25th W			
	26th–last X			
III	Total . . ▶			
IV	Total for quarter (add lines I, II, and III) . .		Column b total must equal line 13	
V	Final deposit made for quarter. (Enter 0 if included in line IV.)			

If you are not liable for returns in the future, write "FINAL" . . . . . ▶

Date final wages paid . . ▶

1 Number of employees (except household) employed in the pay period that includes March 12th (complete first quarter only) . . . . ▶

2 Total wages and tips subject to withholding, plus other compensation . . . . .

3 Total income tax withheld from wages, tips, annuities, sick pay, gambling, etc . .

4 Adjustment of withheld income tax for preceding quarters of calendar year . . .

5 Adjusted total of income tax withheld . . . .

6 Taxable FICA wages paid: $ .... times 13.4% equals tax .

7 a Taxable tips reported: $ .... times 6.7% equals tax .

b Tips deemed to be wages (see instructions): $ .... times 6.7% equals tax .

8 Total FICA taxes (add lines 6, 7a, and 7b) . . . . .

9 Adjustment of FICA taxes (see instructions) . . . .

10 Adjusted total of FICA taxes .

11 Total taxes (add lines 5 and 10) . . . .

12 Advance earned income credit (EIC) payments, if any . .

13 Net taxes (subtract line 12 from line 11) . . . . .

14 Total deposits for quarter. Add lines IV and V, column d, and enter here . . . . ▶

15 Undeposited taxes due (subtract line 14 from line 13). Enter here and pay to Internal Revenue Service . ▶

16 If line 14 is more than line 13, enter overpayment here ▶ $ and check if to be: ☐ Applied to next return, or ☐ Refunded.

Under penalties of perjury, I declare that I have examined this return, including accompanying schedules and statements, and to the best of my knowledge and belief it is true, correct, and complete.

Signature ▶ Title ▶ Date ▶

Please file this form with your Internal Revenue Service Center (see instructions on "Where to File"). Form 941 (Rev. 1-82)

FIGURE 9.7. Every employer must file this quarterly return, Form 941, for federal withholding and social security taxes.

City and state withholding taxes may be payable monthly, semimonthly, quarterly, semiannually, or annually.

Reminders should be entered on your calendar to compute tax totals and prepare and file forms on time. Failure to do this will result in penalties and interest payments.

W-2 FORMS

At the end of the year, you're required to fill out a W-2 form (Figure 9.8) for every employee, listing the total wages, withholding, FICA, and other tax deductions from salary (do not include employer's share of FICA). Copies are provided to the employee, plus city, state, and federal tax agencies. The Internal Revenue Service requires a transmittal Form W-3 to be sent with copies of the W-2 forms.

RECORDING PAYROLL EXPENSES

The simplest way to record payroll expenses is to set up an account in your General Ledger called "Payroll Expenses" and charge all salaries and tax payments to it. Whenever you write a payroll check or make a tax payment, list it in your Cash Disbursements Journal as shown in Figure 9.9. At the end of the month these amounts will all be debited to Payroll Expense in your General Ledger. This simple method is used if you're on a cash basis of accounting for tax purposes.

1 Control number	22222		
2 Employer's name, address, and ZIP code		3 Employer's identification number	4 Employer's State number
		5 Stat. employee ☐ Deceased ☐ Pension plan ☐ Legal rep. ☐	942 emp. ☐ Sub-total ☐ Correction ☐ Void ☐
		6	7 Advance EIC payment
8 Employee's social security number	9 Federal income tax withheld	10 Wages, tips, other compensation	11 FICA tax withheld
12 Employee's name, address, and ZIP code		13 FICA wages	14 FICA tips
		16 Employer's use	
		17 State income tax / 18 State wages, tips, etc.	19 Name of State
		20 Local income tax / 21 Local wages, tips, etc.	22 Name of locality

Form **W-2 Wage and Tax Statement 1981** Copy D For employer Department of the Treasury Internal Revenue Service

FIGURE 9.8. W-2 form which must be completed for each employee at the end of the year.

CASH DISBURSEMENTS JOURNAL Page 1

	date	payee	check# (1)	total (2)	purchase (3)	payroll (4)	general (5)	gen. acct name (6)
1	1 14	J. Jones	1245	342 50		342 50		
2		M. Smith	1246	124 70		124 70		
3		L. Harrison	1247	320 65		320 65		
4	1 16	IRS	1248	232 50		232 50		
5								
6								
7								
8								
9								
10								
11								
12								
13								
14								
15								
16								
17								
18								
19								
20								

FIGURE 9.9. List payroll checks and payroll taxes paid in your Cash Disbursements Journal. Debit to Payroll Expense and credit to Cash.

If you're on the accrual basis of accounting for tax purposes, you use the above method and make an end-of-the-year adjustment for any salaries or tax expenses incurred but not paid by the end of the year. To do this, an account called "Salaries and Taxes Payable" is set up in your General Ledger. If, for example, you owe $250 in salaries and taxes for three days worked in 1996 (for which employees will be paid in 1997), plus $103 in federal withholding and FICA for the last quarter of 1996, plus $98 in unemployment taxes for the whole year of 1996, you would make an entry in your General Journal as shown in Figure 9.10. The total amount of $451.00 ($250 + $103 + $98) would be debited to Payroll Expense and credited to Salaries and Payroll Taxes Payable in your General Ledger.

The $451 would thereby be included as part of 1996's Payroll Expense on your Income Statement and the credit balance of $451 in the Salaries and Payroll Taxes Payable account will be listed as a liability on your Balance Sheet. At the beginning of the following year, you would reverse this entry,

GENERAL JOURNAL Page 2

	date		description	debit ①	credit ②
1	12	31	Payroll Expense	451	
2			Salaries & Payroll Taxes Payable		451
3			Accrued Salaries (250) with.		
4			Taxes (103) & Unemp. Taxes (98)		
5					
6					
7					
8					
9					
10					
11					
12					
13					
14					
15					
16					
17					
18					
19					
20					

FIGURE 9.10. General Journal entry illustrating an end-of-the-year adjustment for wages and payroll taxes owed.

GENERAL JOURNAL Page 2

	date	description	① debit	② credit
1	1 1	Salaries & Payroll Taxes Payable	451	
2		Payroll Expense		451
3		To reverse Accrued Salaries &		
4		Payroll Tax Expense		
5				
6				
7				
8				
9				
10				
11				
12				
13				
14				
15				
16				
17				
18				
19				
20				

FIGURE 9.11. The entry in Figure 9.10 should be reversed at the beginning of the following year.

as illustrated in Figure 9.11, and continue recording payroll expenses in the simple cash method as described above.

STRICT ACCRUAL METHOD OF ACCOUNTING FOR PAYROLL EXPENSES

The strict accrual method is the most complicated; however, at any one time you will know exactly what you owe in payroll taxes.

With this method you'll need four accounts in your General Ledger: Salaries Expense, Payroll Tax Expense, Payroll Taxes Payable, and a Payroll Clearing account. When you compute your employees' salaries in your payroll book, you'll post the total net salaries paid as a credit in the Payroll Clearing account and a debit in the Salaries Expense account. Total withholding plus employees' share of FICA taxes will be credited to Payroll Taxes Payable and debited to Salaries Expense. Employer's share of FICA will be credited to Payroll Taxes Payable and debited to Payroll Tax Expense.

When you write employees' checks, you'll credit Cash and debit the Payroll Clearing account. When you make a tax payment, you'll debit Payroll Taxes Payable and credit Cash.

To illustrate this recording process, let's say you have an employee, Mark Smith, who earns a gross salary of $100. His deductions for federal withholding are $15.00 and for FICA $5.85, or a total deduction of $20.85. Your tax liability (employer's share of FICA) is $5.85. You post from your payroll book as follows:

PAYROLL CLEARING

debit	credit
	79.15

PAYROLL TAXES PAYABLE

debit (−)	credit (+)
	20.85
	5.85

SALARIES EXPENSE

debit (+)	credit (−)
79.15	
20.85	

PAYROLL TAX EXPENSE

debit (+)	credit (−)
5.85	

When you write the employee's check for $79.15, you post from your Cash Disbursements Journal as follows:

CASH

debit (+)	credit (−)
	79.15

PAYROLL CLEARING

debit	credit
79.15	79.15 *

* Prior entry.

When you make the $26.70 total tax payment (employee's share of $20.85 plus your share of $5.85), you post this amount from your Cash Disbursements Journal as follows:

CASH

debit (+)	credit (−)
	79.15 *
	26.70

PAYROLL TAXES PAYABLE

debit (−)	credit (+)
26.70	20.85 *
	5.85 *

* Prior entries.

At the end of the year, the debit balances in Salaries Expense and Payroll Tax Expense will appear on your Income Statement. The credit balance in Payroll Taxes Payable will be listed as a liability on your Balance Sheet. The Payroll Clearing account will always zero out after posting from the Cash Disbursements Journal. If employees earned monies before the end of the year for which they were not paid that year, you can handle this accrued expense as explained in Chapter 11.

DISABILITY AND WORKERS' COMPENSATION

As an employer, you'll probably be required to provide workers' compensation and disability insurance for your employees. This insurance provides payments for medical care in job-related injuries, plus partial salary benefits while employees are out of work due to these injuries. Employer insurance payments are usually based on the number of employees, level of danger in that particular line of work, etc. Your insurance agent can tell you what the requirements are in your state and how much coverage will cost.

You can record payments for workers' compensation and disability insurance in an Insurance Expense account or in your Payroll Expense account in your General Ledger. It makes more sense to include these payments as part of Payroll Expense, however, since they would not be necessary if you did not have employees.

OWNER'S SALARY

If your business is a corporation, you'll include your salary as a regular Payroll expense, taking the necessary tax deductions, etc. If you are a sole proprietor, your withdrawals from the business are not considered part of Payroll expenses, so you set up an account called "Owner's Withdrawal" and post all monies paid to yourself as a debit to this account. At the end of the year, the debit balance in Owner's Withdrawal will be subtracted from Net Earnings to get Retained Earnings (see Chapter 11). If you have a partnership, each partner will have a Withdrawal account in which to list monies paid to him or her by the business. (See more details on this in Chapter 16 on Partnership Accounting.)

Money taken out of a business by a sole proprietor or partners will not have tax deductions taken for income and social security taxes. You, as an individual, will be responsible for paying Estimated Income Taxes and Self-Employment Social Security Taxes. Your Internal Revenue Service agent or Internal Revenue Publication 17, *Your Federal Income Tax for Individuals,* can give you further information on this.

SUMMING UP

As an employer, you have a number of obligations for insurance coverage, tax withholding and payment, and filing various forms. You can't consider money withheld from employees' salaries as part of your company's capital. Reserves should be kept to cover payroll taxes and payments should be made promptly. The Internal Revenue Service has a strong hand, which includes the right not only to levy penalties for lateness, but to actually close down your business for failure to pay payroll taxes.

10

Sales Taxes

Many states have sales and use taxes that a seller must collect from consumers and pay periodically. The tax rate will often vary from county to county within the state. Products and services subject to sales and use taxes will vary from state to state. For example, in New Jersey clothing is exempt from sales tax, whereas in New York State it's taxed.

You should write to your state government and ask for information on sales and use tax laws in your state. The first step is usually to obtain a seller's permit. These permits or certificates must be prominently displayed at your place of business.

COLLECTING SALES TAXES

If you use sales slips, you must compute the sales tax and list the amount of tax separately from the total purchase amount. When using a cash register, a subtotal of the purchases is taken, then the tax is added. Figure 10.1 shows a "Sales Tax Collection Schedule" provided by the State of New Jersey to help sellers compute sales taxes. If you neglect to collect these taxes as required by law, you're still required to pay them.

RESALE CERTIFICATES

Items that are sold for resale are normally exempt from sales and use taxes. For this reason, wholesalers and manufacturers who sell their products to retailers (who will "resell" them) do not collect sales taxes. Even if you're a retailer, you may occasionally have a commerical customer who presents you with a resale certificate in order to exempt the purchase from taxation. A New York State resale certificate is shown in Figure 10.2

When you purchase supplies, etc., you may have to present a resale certificate to your supplier in order to exempt the purchase from sales taxes. Your state's regulations should be studied carefully. For example, in one state, inner packaging materials are exempt, but outer packaging cartons are

STATE OF NEW JERSEY
DEPARTMENT OF THE TREASURY
Division of Taxation

SALES TAX COLLECTION SCHEDULE

RATE: 5% **EFFECTIVE MARCH 1, 1970**

Amount of Sale	Tax to be Collected	Amount of Sale	Tax to be Collected
\$0.01 to \$0.10 . . .	None	\$6.11 to \$6.25 . .	\$0.31
0.11 to 0.25 . . .	1¢	6.26 to 6.46 . .	.32
0.26 to 0.46 . . .	2¢	6.47 to 6.67 . .	.33
0.47 to 0.67 . . .	3¢	6.68 to 6.88 . . .	.34
0.68 to 0.88 . . .	4¢	6.89 to 7.10 . . .	.35
0.89 to 1.10 . . .	5¢	7.11 to 7.25 . . .	.36
1.11 to 1.25 . . .	6¢	7.26 to 7.46 . . .	.37
1.26 to 1.46 . . .	7¢	7.47 to 7.67 . . .	.38
1.47 to 1.67 . . .	8¢	7.68 to 7.88 . . .	.39
1.68 to 1.88 . . .	9¢	7.89 to 8.10 . . .	.40
1.89 to 2.10 . . .	\$0.10	8.11 to 8.25 . . .	.41
2.11 to 2.25 . . .	.11	8.26 to 8.46 . . .	.42
2.26 to 2.46 . . .	.12	8.47 to 8.67 . . .	.43
2.47 to 2.67 . . .	.13	8.68 to 8.88 . . .	.44
2.68 to 2.88 . . .	.14	8.89 to 9.10 . . .	.45
2.89 to 3.10 . . .	.15	9.11 to 9.25 . . .	.46
3.11 to 3.25 . . .	.16	9.26 to 9.46 . . .	.47
3.26 to 3.46 . . .	.17	9.47 to 9.67 . . .	.48
3.47 to 3.67 . . .	.18	9.68 to 9.88 . . .	.49
3.68 to 3.88 . . .	.19	9.89 to 10.00 . . .	.50
3.89 to 4.10 . . .	.20	Over \$10	.50*
4.11 to 4.25 . . .	.21	Over 20	1.00*
4.26 to 4.46 . . .	.22	Over 30	1.50*
4.47 to 4.67 . . .	.23	Over 40	2.00*
4.68 to 4.88 . . .	.24	Over 50	2.50*
4.89 to 5.10 . . .	.25	Over 60	3.00*
5.11 to 5.25 . . .	.26	Over 70	3.50*
5.26 to 5.46 . . .	.27	Over 80	4.00*
5.47 to 5.67 . . .	.28	Over 90	4.50*
5.68 to 5.88 . . .	.29	Over 100	5.00*
5.89 to 6.10 . . .	.30	Over 200	10.00*

*On amounts above \$10.00, the tax shall be \$0.05 on each full dollar of the amount of sale, plus the tax on each part of a dollar in excess of a full dollar in accordance with the above formula.

ST-75 (3-70) IBM Z26018 23721 PRINTED IN U.S.A.

FIGURE 10.1. Most states provide a sales tax collection schedule such as this one to help compute sales taxes.

not. If you have any questions, your local sales tax office will supply the answers.

COMPUTING SALES TAXES

If *all* your sales are subject to sales tax and a separate accounting for sales tax collections is not required by law, you can use the following method to compute your sales taxes when due:

1. Divide total sales (including taxes collected) by one plus the sales tax rate to get the sales-only figure.

ST-120 (1/72)

State of New York - Department of Taxation and Finance - Sales Tax Bureau

New York State and Local Sales and Use Tax

To be completed by purchaser and given to and retained by vendor.

Read Instructions on back of this certificate.

RESALE CERTIFICATE

The vendor must collect the tax on a sale of taxable property or services unless the purchaser gives him a properly completed resale certificate or exemption certificate.

NAME OF VENDOR			DATE
STREET ADDRESS			*Check Applicable Box* ☐ Single Purchase Certificate ☐ Blanket Certificate
CITY	STATE	ZIP CODE	

The undersigned hereby certifies that he:

holds a valid Certificate of Authority to collect New York State and local sales and use tax.

is principally engaged in *(indicate nature of business)*..

....

intends that the *(check applicable box or boxes)*

A. ☐ tangible personal property is for resale in its present form or as a component part of tangible personal property.

B. ☐ tangible personal property is for use in performing taxable services where such property becomes a component part of the tangible personal property upon which the services are performed or will be actually transferred to the purchaser of the service in conjunction with the performance of the service.

C. ☐ service is for resale.

D. ☐ shipping cartons, containers and other packaging material are for resale. (see special information on shipping cartons, etc. on reverse side.)

understands that this certificate may not be used to purchase items or services which are not for resale and that he will pay the use tax on tangible personal property or services purchased pursuant to this certificate and subsequently used or consumed in a taxable manner, and that any erroneous or false use of this certificate will subject him to payment of tax plus penalties and interest.

SIGNATURE OF OWNER, PARTNER, OFFICER OF CORPORATION, ETC.	NAME OF PURCHASER		
TITLE	STREET ADDRESS		
Certificate of Authority Identification Number of Purchaser	CITY	STATE	ZIP CODE

FIGURE 10.2. New York State resale certificate, which is filed by the purchaser to exempt purchases from sales taxes.

2. Multiply the sales-only figure by the sales tax rate to get the sales tax. For example,

Total sales: $8,882.50
Tax rate: 4.5 percent

$8,882.50 ÷ 1.045 = $8,500 sales only
$8,500 x .045 = $382.50 sales tax

Check:

$8,500 + $382.50 = $8,882.50 total sales

If only *part* of your sales are subject to sales and use taxes, you should record taxable sales and tax collections separately, and keep a sales tax record as illustrated in Figure 10.3. At the end of the month, total taxable sales and sales taxes; make a sales tax payment if required. At the end of the quarter, compute totals for that period and transfer to tax returns.

PAYING SALES TAXES

You will probably be required to pay sales taxes quarterly or monthly, and file a return quarterly. For example, in New Jersey you must pay taxes quarterly unless your sales and use tax liability for the first two months of a quarter exceeds $100 per month, in which case you must pay them monthly. A sample of the monthly remittance statement is shown in Figure 10.4. The quarterly return is shown in Figure 10.5.

There are penalties for failing to file returns, or filing late, so you must be sure to comply with legal deadlines. Generally, even if you don't have any

SALES TAX RECORD

date	total sales	taxable sales	collected taxes

FIGURE 10.3. A Sales Tax Record such as this one can be used if all your sales aren't subject to sales tax.

82

STATE OF NEW JERSEY
SALES AND USE TAX
MONTHLY REMITTANCE STATEMENT

FOR THE MONTH OF **APRIL, 1982**

THIS STATEMENT DUE **MAY 20, 1982**

IMPORTANT—PLEASE READ CAREFULLY—If your sales and use tax liability for the month exceeds $100, you must complete and forward this statement together with check or money order for the amount due to the DIVISION OF TAXATION on or before the DUE DATE indicated above. Willful failure to file this statement on or before the due date may result in a fine of $500 or imprisonment for up to six months, or both.

1

IF THE NAME AND/OR ADDRESS BELOW IS INCORRECT, MAKE THE NECESSARY CHANGES AND ADD POSTAL ZIP CODE

1	AMOUNT OF TAX DUE (SEE INSTRUCTIONS)	
2	PENALTY AND INTEREST (SEE INSTRUCTIONS)	
3	TOTAL AMOUNT DUE (LINE 1 PLUS LINE 2)	

T-222-235-318/000 2 INFO
INFORMATION PLUS INC
LYN TAETZSCH
1165 LONG HILL RD
STIRLING NJ 07980

4

MAKE CHECK OR MONEY ORDER PAYABLE TO:
NEW JERSEY SALES TAX
CN 999
TRENTON NEW JERSEY 08646

PAY THIS AMOUNT

I CERTIFY THAT ALL INFORMATION ON THIS STATEMENT IS CORRECT.

SIGNATURE TITLE DATE

ST-51 (1-82) SEE REVERSE SIDE

AVOID PENALTIES — FILE ON TIME

FIGURE 10.4. Monthly remittance statement for the State of New Jersey.

taxable sales in a particular period, you're still required to file a return. You should check the laws in your state carefully.

RECORDING SALES TAX PAYMENTS

If you're on the cash basis of accounting for tax purposes (see Chapter 2), you should record sales tax payments when you pay them—that is, enter the

82

STATE OF NEW JERSEY
SALES AND USE TAX
QUARTERLY RETURN

FOR QUARTER ENDING **JUNE, 1982**

THIS RETURN DUE **JULY 20, 1982**

MAKE CHECKS OR MONEY ORDERS PAYABLE TO:
NEW JERSEY SALES TAX
CN 999
TRENTON, NEW JERSEY 08646

IMPORTANT: PLEASE READ CAREFULLY

1. This return must be filed with the New Jersey Division of Taxation even though no tax is payable or no sales were made.
2. Change in ownership or organization requires a new Certificate of Authority. Do not use previous owner's tax return to file your return.
3. Complete reverse side of this form.

5

IF THE BUSINESS TO WHICH THIS RETURN IS ADDRESSED WILL NOT FILE FUTURE RETURNS, GIVE REASON:

IF THE NAME AND/OR ADDRESS BELOW IS INCORRECT, MAKE THE NECESSARY CHANGES AND ADD POSTAL ZIP CODE

T-222-235-318/000 2 INFO
INFORMATION PLUS INC
LYN TAETZSCH
1165 LONG HILL RD
STIRLING NJ 07980

6

IF BUSINESS WAS SOLD OR OWNERSHIP WAS CHANGED GIVE NAME & ADDRESS (INCLUDING ZIP CODE) OF NEW OWNER(S):

NAME
ADDRESS
CITY & STATE
ZIP CODE
DATE BUSINESS WAS TRANSFERRED

ST-50 (1-82) SEE REVERSE SIDE

FIGURE 10.5. The front and back of a quarterly sales and use tax return for the State of New Jersey.

6-82

NEW JERSEY SALES AND USE TAX

QUARTERLY RETURN

READ ALL INSTRUCTIONS BEFORE COMPLETING THIS RETURN. CHECK YOUR COMPUTATIONS.

1	GROSS RECEIPTS FOR APR., MAY, JUNE	
2	LESS: DEDUCTION (SEE INSTRUCTIONS)	
3	BALANCE SUBJECT TO SALES TAX (LINE 1 MINUS LINE 2)	
4	A 5% OF LINE 3	
	B SALES TAX COLLECTED	
5	AMOUNT OF SALES TAX DUE (ENTER GREATER OF LINE 4A OR 4B)	
6	ADD: AMOUNT OF USE TAX DUE (SEE INSTRUCTIONS)	
7	TOTAL TAX DUE (ADD LINES 5 AND 6)	
	If you have paid part of your tax liability for the quarter covered by this return in the form of monthly remittances COMPLETE LINE 8	
8	LESS: MONTHLY PAYMENTS FIRST MONTH SECOND MONTH	
	TOTAL →	
9	QUARTERLY AMOUNT DUE (LINE 7 MINUS LINE 8)	
10	ADD: PENALTY AND INTEREST (SEE INSTRUCTIONS)	
11	ADJUSTED AMOUNT DUE (LINE 9 PLUS LINE 10) PAY THIS AMOUNT	

I CERTIFY THAT ALL INFORMATION ON THIS RETURN IS CORRECT.

SIGNATURE TITLE DATE

FIGURE 10.5. (Continued.)

payment as usual in your Cash Disbursements Journal as illustrated in Figure 10.6. This figure will then be posted to an account called "Sales and Use Tax Expense" as illustrated in Figure 10.7. At the end of the year, the debit balance in Sales and Use Tax Expense will be listed as an operating expense on your Income Statement (see Chapter 11).

If you're on the accrual basis of accounting for tax purposes, you should use the above recording method and make an adjustment at the end of the year. If, for example, you owe $68 in sales taxes for the final quarter of the year but have not yet made the actual payment, you make an entry in your

CASH DISBURSEMENTS JOURNAL Page 3

	date		payee	check# ①	total ②	salaries ③	purchase ④	general ⑤	gen.acct name ⑥
1	3	14	N.Y.S. Sales Tax Bureau	3025	45 32			45 32	Sales Tax Ex.
2									
3									
4									
5									
6									
7									
8									
9									
10									
11									
12									
13									
14									
15									
16									
17									
18									
19									
20									

FIGURE 10.6. Page from a Cash Disbursements Journal illustrating the entry of a sales tax payment.

SALES AND USE TAX EXPENSE

DATE 19__		ITEMS	FOLIO	√	DEBITS		DATE 19__		ITEMS	FOLIO	√	CREDITS	
3	14	1st Quarter Tax Pmt.	CD-3		45	32							

FIGURE 10.7. The $45.32 sales tax payment from Figure 10.6 is shown here posted as a debit to the Sales and Use Tax Expense General Ledger account.

GENERAL JOURNAL Page 2

	date		description	debit ①	credit ②
1	12	31	Sales & Use Tax Ex.	68 00	
2			Sales & Use Taxes Payable		68 00
3			Adjustment for 4th		
4			quarter Taxes Owed		
5					
6					
7					
8					
9					
10					
11					
12					
13					
14					
15					
16					
17					
18					
19					
20					
21					
22					
23					

FIGURE 10.8. General Journal entry illustrating an end-of-the-year adjustment for sales and use taxes owed.

General Journal as illustrated in Figure 10.8. When these figures are posted to your General Ledger accounts, your Sales and Use Tax Expense account will be increased (debited) by $68 and your Sales and Use Tax Payable account will show a credit balance of $68. This will appear as a liability on your Balance Sheet.

At the beginning of the following year, after the expense accounts have been cleared (see Chapter 11), this entry is reversed as shown in Figure 10.9. You then continue recording sales taxes when paid, as in the cash method discussed above. (Note that this $68 will be subtracted from the debit balance in the Sales and Use Tax Expense account because it was already expensed the previous year.)

GENERAL JOURNAL Page 2

	date	description	debit ①	credit ②
1	1 1	Sales & Use Taxes Payable	68 00	
2		Sales & Use Taxes Expense		68 00
3		To reverse end-of-year		
4		Adjustment		
5				
6				
7				
8				
9				
10				
11				
12				
13				
14				
15				
16				
17				
18				
19				
20				
21				
22				
23				
24				
25				
26				
27				
28				
29				
30				

FIGURE 10.9. The General Journal entry from Figure 10.8 must be reversed at the beginning of the following year.

SUMMING UP

If your state requires the collection of sales and use taxes on various products and services, you must find out how the law affects your business activities and apply for a seller's permit if necessary. Taxes must be collected and a record kept of taxable sales in your Daily Summary or a Sales Tax Record, unless your total sales are taxed at a single rate. Tax payments must be made and returns filed on time in order to avoid fines and penalties.

Sales tax payments must be recorded in an expense account in your General Ledger. If you're on the accrual basis of accounting for tax purposes, you can make an end-of-the-year adjustment to include taxes owed for the final month or quarter.

11

Preparing Financial Statements

The first step in preparing financial statements is to prepare a trial balance of your General Ledger accounts. Once the debit and credit totals balance, you'll then make any necessary adjustments for accrued expenses, prepaid expenses, write-off of bad debts, depreciation, and inventories. After these adjustments are made, the final debit and credit balances for each account will be used in compiling the Income Statement and the Balance Sheet.

Examples are given in this chapter of financial statements for various types of businesses such as service, retail, and manufacturing. The statements of wholesalers who warehouse inventories will be set up similarly to those of a retail store, since purchasing inventories for resale will be the basis of their profit making.

Since the largest percentage of small businesses are sole proprietorships, most of the sample financial statements in this chapter are for proprietorships. One set of statements has been included, however, to illustrate a corporation's Income Statement and Balance Sheet. Partnership statements are illustrated in Chapter 16 on Partnership Accounting.

MONTHLY TRIAL BALANCE

At the end of every month (after all posting is completed) you should total figures in each account in your General Ledger. In asset and expense accounts, this means taking a debit balance by subtracting the credit column from the debit column total (Figure 11.1). In Liability, Owner's Equity, and Income (Sales or Revenues) accounts, a credit balance is taken by subtracting the debit column total from the credit column total (Figure 11.2). All asset and expense accounts will not always have a debit balance. For example, if you have overdrawn your cash (written checks for more than you have in the bank), you'll have a credit balance in Cash. Likewise, all liability and expense accounts may not always have credit balances.

CASH

DATE 19___		ITEMS		FOLIO	√	DEBITS	DATE 19___		ITEMS	FOLIO	√	CREDITS
		PREVIOUS BAL.				12325						
1	31	Jan. Receipts	12,525	CR-1		6450	1	31	Jan. Disbursements			6250
						18775						
2	29	Feb. "	9,371	CR-1		5278	2	29	Feb. "			8432
						24053						14682
3	31	Mar. "	10,692	CR-2		7056	3	31	Mar. "			5735
						31109						20417
4	30	Apr. "	12,496	CR-2		6023	4	30	Apr. "			4219
						37132						24636
5	31	May "	* 9,795	CR-2		4034	5	31	May "			6735
						41166						31371

*This is the balance in this account at May 31.

FIGURE 11.1. Monthly debit balances are written to the left of the debit folio in this cash account.

ACCOUNTS PAYABLE

DATE 19___		ITEMS	FOLIO	√	DEBITS	DATE 19___		ITEMS		FOLIO	√	CREDITS
1	31	Jan. Payments	CD-1		405	1	31	Jan. Previous Bal Purchases	5,325	PJ-1		2705 3025
2	29	Feb. "	CD-1		2176 2681	2	29	Feb. "	4,022	PJ-1		5730 873
3	31	Mar. "	CD-2		1052 3683	3	31	Mar. "	4,376	PJ-2		6603 1406
4	30	Apr. "	CD-3		542 4175	4	30	Apr. "	12,559	PJ-2		8009 8725
5	31	May "	CD-3		1607 5982	5	31	May "	* 14,816	PJ-3		16734 3864 20598

*This is the balance in this account at May 31.

FIGURE 11.2. In Liability, Owner's Equity, and Income accounts, take a credit balance.

Every account balance from your General Ledger is listed on a Trial Balance Worksheet as shown in Figure 11.3. The figures in each column are then added and the totals compared. They should match.

If the debit and credit column totals don't match, you've made an error somewhere and must find it: First add the columns again on your trial balance; then double check that you have copied the correct amounts from your General Ledger; then check the addition and subtraction in each General Ledger account. If you still haven't found the error, you should go back to sources (General Journal, Cash Receipts Journal, Cash Disbursements Journal, Sales Journal, Purchases Journal) to make sure figures were

XYZ COMPANY

Trial Balance As of 10/31/95

	General Ledger Balance	
	Debit	Credit
Cash	31246 -	
Petty Cash Fund	50 -	
Accounts Receivable	12043 -	
Deposits	100 -	
Fixed Assets	43056 -	
Accumulated Depreciation		12347 -
Accounts Payable		2310 -
Notes Payable		30846 -
Owners Capital		20000 -
Retained Earnings		19216 -
Sales		85432 -
Misc. Revenues		5076 -
Purchases Expenses	40144 -	
Salaries Expenses	21067 -	
Rent Expense	8700 -	
Utilities Expense	403 -	
Advertising Expense	3725 -	
Supplies Expense	315 -	
Bad Debt Expense	403 -	
Insurance Expense	672 -	
Misc. Expense	803 -	
Owner's Withdrawal	12500 -	
	175227 -	175227 -

FIGURE 11.3. Monthly Trial Balance Worksheet.

posted accurately, and that the total of the entries from each source zeroes out.

ACCRUALS AND ADJUSTMENTS

At least once a year, but possibly as often as each month, you'll want to make the accruals and adjustments necessary to prepare financial statements. If you prepare statements each month, the adjustments should only be made on the trial balance worksheet, not in the General Journal and General Ledger. Accruals and other such adjustments should only be recorded in these ledgers at the end of the year. The kinds of adjustments you'll make will depend on the nature of your business and whether you use the cash or accrual basis of accounting.

Cash Basis

If you use the cash basis of accounting, the only adjustments you will probably need to make are to record depreciation expense if you have fixed assets (see Chapter 8) and to correct any errors you've made.

Accrual Basis

If you use the accrual basis of accounting, you must record all income and expenses in the accounting period in which you *earned* the income or *incurred* the expenses. Let's assume you're preparing financial statements for the year ended December 31, 1995. You must make any adjustments necessary to reflect all business taken place prior to that date. Some adjustments you might want to make are:

Accounts Payable Accrual. If you use the simplified accrual method of recording purchases and accounts payable, you should make an adjustment to record unpaid invoices as described in Chapter 5. The entry will be a debit to various expense accounts and a credit to accounts payable.

Expense Accrual. An accrual should be made for any goods or services you received before year end even if you haven't received an invoice by the time you prepare financial statements. Examples would be money owed to employees for days worked, lawyer's fees or telephone service you haven't been billed for.

Suppose, for example, the year ends on Wednesday and you pay your employees on Friday. When preparing the end of year financial statements, you have to make an accrual for the three days' payroll expense incurred.

Let's assume you have three employees who each earn $300 per week. They have worked three-fifths of the week. Therefore, you should accrue $540 (3/5 of $900). You would make an entry in the General Journal debiting Payroll Expense and crediting Salaries Payable.

Payroll and Sales Taxes. Make sure you make an entry to record a liability for any amounts owed to government agencies as of the end of the year.

Recording Depreciation. If you have capitalized fixed assets, you will have to make an adjustment to record depreciation expense. See Chapter 8 for how to do this.

Prepaid Expenses. If you have a significant amount of supplies on hand at the end of the year, you might want to count up and value your supplies and capitalize them. This is done by debiting Prepaid Expense (an asset account) and crediting Supplies Expense (an expense account).

Writing Off Bad Debts. At least once a year you should evaluate the collectibility of your accounts receivable and record an entry to write off any bad debts (see Chapters 6 and 7).

Any required adjustments should be posted to the General Journal as illustrated below:

	debit	*credit*
(1)		
Prepaid Expenses	150	
Supplies Expense		150
To record supplies on hand at 12/31/95		
(2)		
Salaries Expense	540	
Salaries Payable		540
To record salaries from 12/29/95 to 12/31/95		
(3)		
Salaries Expense	230	
Payroll Taxes Payable		230
To record federal withholding and FICA expense thru 12/31/95		

	debit	*credit*
(4)		
Sales Tax Expense	150	
Sales Taxes Payable		150
To record sales taxes owed on merchandise sold as of 12/31/95		
(5)		
Bad Debt Expense	300	
Accounts Receivable		300
To write off invoice # 1029—not collectible		
(6)		
Depreciation Expense	1234	
Accumulated Depreciation		1234
To record depreciation expense for the year		

All of the above adjustments should be posted to the General Ledger accounts and to the Trial Balance as illustrated in Figure 11.4. The final figures in the Adjusted Trial Balance columns on your Trial Balance Worksheet should match the final debit and credit balances in your General Ledger. All of the above adjusting Journal entries except number 6 (depreciation) should be reversed at the beginning of the following year. This is explained later in this chapter.

INCOME STATEMENT AND BALANCE SHEET

Separate the Income Statement and Balance Sheet figures on your Trial Balance Worksheet as shown in Figure 11.5. The revenues and expense accounts will appear on your Income Statement, as illustrated in Figure 11.6. Operating expenses are deducted from revenues to get the profit (earnings) or loss. Owner's Withdrawals are deducted from this figure to get Retained Earnings (money that will remain in the business as working capital).

The retained earnings for the year will be added to the previous balance in that account (see "Closing Out Income Statement Accounts" below) and the new total will appear on the Balance Sheet (Figure 11.7). Asset accounts such as Cash, Prepaid Expenses, Deposits, Machinery and Equipment, etc., will

XYZ COMPANY

Trial Balance As of 12/31/95

	General Ledger Balance		Adjustments		Adjusted Trial Balance	
	Debit	Credit	Debit	Credit	Debit	Credit
Cash	6400 -					
Petty Cash	100 -					
Change Fund	50 -					
TOTAL CASH	6550 -				6550 -	
Deposits	100 -				100 -	
Prepaid Expenses			150 (1)		150 -	
Accounts Rec.	6420 -			300 (5)	6120 -	
Notes Rec.	540 -				540 -	
Fixed Assets	32500 -				32500 -	
Accum Dep.		9750 -		1234 - (6)		9984 -
Accounts Payable		346 -				346 -
Notes Payable		11054 -				11054 -
Salaries Payable				540 (2)		540 -
Payroll Taxes Payable				230 (3)		230 -
Sales Taxes Payable				150 - (4)		150 -
Owner's Capital		12200 -				12200 -
Retained Earnings		9935 -				9935 -
Sales		65425 -				65425 -
Misc. Revenues		540 -				540 -
Salaries Ex.	42832 -		540 - (2) 230 - (3)		43602 -	
Rent Ex.	2900 -				2900 -	
Interest Ex.	138 -				138 -	
Promotion Ex.	1300 -				1300 -	
Bad Debt Ex.	230 -		300 (5)		530 -	
Sales Tax Ex.	200 -		150 (4)		350 -	
Depreciation Ex.			1234 (6)		1234 -	
Supplies Ex.	540 -			150 - (1)	390 -	
Owners Withdrawal	14000 -				14000 -	
	108250 -	108250 -	2604 -	2604 -	110404 -	110404 -

FIGURE 11.4. Year-end Trial Balance Worksheet with adjustments.

XYZ COMPANY

Trial Balance As of 12/31/95

	General Ledger Bal.		Adjustments		Adjusted Trial Bal.		Income Statement		Balance Sheet	
	1	2	3	4	5	6	7	8	9	10
	Debit	Credit	Debit	Credit	Debit	Credit	Debit	Credit	Debit	Credit
Cash	6400 -									
Petty Cash	100 -									
Change Fund	50 -									
TOTAL CASH	6550 -				6550 -				6550 -	
Deposits	100 -				100 -				100 -	
Prepaid Expenses			150 - (1)		150 -				150 -	
Accounts Rec.	6420 -			300 - (5)	6120 -				6120 -	
Notes Rec.	540 -				540 -				540 -	
Fixed Assets	32500 -				32500 -				32500 -	
Accum. Dep.		8750 -		1234 - (6)		9984 -				9984 -
Accounts Payable		346 -				346 -				346 -
Notes Payable		11054 -				11054				11054 -
Salaries Payable				540 - (2)		540 -				540 -
Payroll Taxes Payable				230 - (3)		230 -				230 -
Sales Taxes Payable				150 - (4)		150 -				150 -
Owners Capital		12200 -				12200 -				12200 -
Retained Earnings		9935 -				9935 -				9935 -
Sales		65425 -				65425 -		65425 -		+ 1521 - 11456 -
Misc. Revenues		540 -				540 -		540 -		
Salaries Ex.	42832 -		540 (2) 230 (3)		43602 -		43602 -			
Rent Ex.	2900 -				2900 -		2900 -			
Interest Ex.	138 -				138 -		138 -			
Promotion Ex.	1300 -				1300 -		1300 -			
Bad Debt Ex.	230 -		300 - (5)		530 -		530 -			
Sales Tax Ex.	200 -		150 - (4)		350 -		350 -			
Depreciation Ex.			1234 - (6)		1234 -		1234 -			
Supplies Ex.	540 -			150 - (1)	390 -		390 -			
Owners Withdrawal	14000 -				14000 -		14000 -			
	108250 -	108250 -	2604 -	2604 -	110404 -	110404 -	64444 -	65965 - (64444 -)	45960 -	45960 -
								1521 -		

FIGURE 11.5. Figures from the Trial Balance Worksheet in Figure 11.4 separated into Income Statement and Balance Sheet accounts.

XYZ COMPANY
INCOME STATEMENT 1/1/95 TO 12/31/95

Sales	$65,425	
Miscellaneous Revenues	540	
Total Revenues		$65,965
Operating Expenses		
Salaries	43,602	
Rent	2,900	
Interest	138	
Promotion	1,300	
Bad Debts	530	
Sales Taxes	350	
Depreciation Expense	1,234	
Supplies Expense	390	
Total Operating Expenses		50,444
Net Earnings		15,521
Less Owner's Withdrawal		14,000
Earnings After Owner's Withdrawal		$ 1,521
Retained Earnings, Beginning of Year		9,935
Retained Earnings, End of Year		$11,456

FIGURE 11.6. Income Statement drawn up from the Trial Balance Worksheet in Figures 11.4 and 11.5.

XYZ COMPANY
BALANCE SHEET AS OF 12/31/95

Assets			*Liabilities*		
Cash		$ 6,550	Accounts Payable		$ 346
Deposits		100	Notes Payable		11,054
Prepaid Expenses		150	Salaries Payable		540
Notes Receivable		540	Payroll Taxes Payable		230
Accounts Receivable		6,120	Sales Taxes Payable		150
			Total Liabilities		12,320
Fixed Assets	32,500				
Less Accumulated					
Depreciation	9,984		*Owner's Equity*		
Total Fixed Assets		22,516	Owner's Capital	12,200	
			Retained Earnings	11,456	
			Total Owner's Equity		23,656
Total Assets		$35,976	*Liabilities + Owner's Equity*		$35,976

FIGURE 11.7. Balance Sheet drawn up from the Trial Balance Worksheet in Figures 11.4 and 11.5.

be listed on the Balance Sheet. Liabilities such as Accounts Payable, Loans Payable, Sales Taxes Payable, etc., will be listed and totaled. You will then list Owner's Capital and the new total in Retained Earnings. When Owner's Equity is added to the Liabilities total, this figure should match the Assets total.

RETAIL AND WHOLESALE FINANCIAL STATEMENTS

If revenues are generated through the sale of purchased inventories, your General Ledger will include an Inventory and Purchases account (see Chapter 12). To prepare your financial statements, you add an account called "Cost of Goods Sold" and list it on your Trial Balance Worksheet as shown in Figure 11.8. As explained in Chapter 12, Cost of Goods Sold is arrived at by adding beginning inventory to purchases and subtracting ending inventory as follows:

Cost of Goods Sold: beginning inventory
+purchases
-ending inventory

The inventory figure in your General Ledger will be beginning inventory. This amount should be debited (added) to Cost of Goods Sold and credited (subtracted) to Inventory (see General Journal entry in Figure 11.9). Then debit the amount in Purchases to Cost of Goods Sold and credit Purchases (Figure 11.10). Finally, take the dollar value of your costed physical inventory at year end (see Chapter 12), credit this ending inventory amount to Cost of Goods Sold, and debit it to Inventory (Figure 11.11).

As illustrated in Figure 11.8, these adjustments to the Trial Balance will give you the new Inventory figure and a Cost of Goods Sold figure. When transferring these figures to your Income Statement, you should show how the Cost of Goods Sold was arrived at, as shown in Figure 11.12. The end-of-year Inventory figure will appear as an asset on the Balance Sheet, as shown in Figure 11.13.

MANUFACTURING FINANCIAL STATEMENTS

If revenues are generated through the sale of manufactured inventories, your General Ledger will include an Inventory and Purchases account. In addition, you'll separate manufacturing labor expense from sales and administrative labor expenses. Before preparing your financial statements, you'll also assign a percentage of general overhead expenses (rent, utilities,

XYZ

Trial Balance

	General Ledger Balance		Adjustments		Adjusted
	Debit	Credit	Debit	Credit	Debit
Cash	3570				3570
Inventory	15500		18000 (6)	15500 (4)	18000
Loans Rec.					
Fixed Assets	51600				51600
Accum. Dep.		10500		1300 (1)	
Accounts Payable		7000			
Notes Payable		10000			
Salaries Payable				200 (2)	
Sales Taxes Payable				450 (3)	
Owner's Capital		23000			
Retained Earnings		10500			
Sales		90000			
Cost of Goods Sold			15500 (4)	18000 (6)	
			55000 (5)		52500
Misc. Revenues		600			
Purchases Ex.	55000			55000 (5)	
Payroll Ex.	15000		200 (2)		15200
Rent Ex.	2400				2400
Advertising Ex.	1500				1500
Sales Tax Ex.	630		450 (3)		1080
Depreciation Ex.			1300 (1)		1300
Misc. Ex.	400				400
Owner's Withdrawal	6000				6000
	151600	151600	90450	90450	153550

FIGURE 11.8. Trial Balance Worksheet for a retail store. Wholesale businesses would be similar, with cost of goods sold computed by adding beginning inventory to purchases and subtracting ending inventory.

RETAIL STORE
AS OF 12/31/78

Trial Balance	Income Statement		Balance Sheet		
Credit	Debit	Credit	Debit	Credit	
			3570		
			18000		
			51600		
11800				11800	
7000				7000	
10000				10000	
200				200	
450				450	
23000				23000	
10500				10500	+ 10,220 = 20,720
90000		90000			
	52500				
600		600			
	15200				
	2400				
	1500				
	1080				
	1300				
	400				
	6000				
153550	80380	90600	73170	73170	
		80380			
		10220			

FIGURE 11.8. (Continued.)

GENERAL JOURNAL Page 2

	date	description	debit ①	credit ②
1	12 31	Cost of Goods Sold	155 00	
2		Inventory		155 00
3		Add Beginning Inventory to		
4		Cost of Goods Sold		
5				
6				
7				
8				
9				
10				

FIGURE 11.9. General Journal entry to transfer beginning inventory to cost of goods sold.

supplies, etc.) to Manufacturing Overhead. Chapter 13 covers these procedures in detail. As explained in Chapter 13, the Cost of Goods Sold in manufacturing is arrived at as follows:

Cost of Goods Sold: beginning inventory
+ purchases
+ manufacturing labor expense
+ manufacturing overhead
− ending inventory

GENERAL JOURNAL Page 2

	date	description	debit ①	credit ②
1	12 31	Cost of Goods Sold	550 00	
2		Purchases		550 00
3		Add Purchases to Cost		
4		of Goods Sold		
5				
6				
7				
8				
9				
10				
11				

FIGURE 11.10. General Journal entry to transfer purchases to cost of goods sold.

GENERAL JOURNAL Page 2

	date		description	debit ①	credit ②
1	12	31	Inventory	18000	
2			Cost of Goods Sold		18000
3			Subtract Ending Inventory		
4			from Cost of Goods Sold		
5					
6					
7					
8					

FIGURE 11.11. General Journal entry to make the Inventory amount show the year-end inventory, and to subtract this inventory from cost of goods sold.

XYZ RETAIL STORE
INCOME STATEMENT FOR 1/1/95 TO 12/31/95

Sales		$90,000
Cost of Goods Sold		
Beginning Inventory	15,500	
Plus Purchases	55,000	
Less Ending Inventory	(18,000)	
Cost of Goods Sold		52,500
Gross Margin		37,500
Miscellaneous Revenues		600
Gross Profit		38,100
Operating Expenses		
Salaries	15,200	
Rent	2,400	
Advertising	1,500	
Sales Taxes	1,080	
Depreciation Expense	1,300	
Miscellaneous Expense	400	
Total Operating Expenses		21,880
Net Earnings		16,220
Less Owner's Withdrawal		6,000
Earnings after Owner's Withdrawal		$10,220
Retained Earnings, Beginning of Year		10,500
Retained Earnings, End of Year		$20,720

FIGURE 11.12. Retail store Income Statement prepared from the Trial Balance Worksheet in Figure 11.8.

XYZ RETAIL STORE
BALANCE SHEET AS OF 12/31/95

Assets			*Liabilities*		
Cash		$ 3,570	Accounts Payable		$ 7,000
Inventory		18,000	Notes Payable		10,000
			Salaries Payable		200
Fixed Assets	51,600		Sales Taxes Payable		450
Less Accumulated			Total Liabilities		17,650
Depreciation	11,800				
Total Fixed Assets		39,800	*Owner's Equity*		
			Owner's Capital	23,000	
			Retained Earnings	20,720	
			Total Owner's Equity		43,720
Total Assets		$61,370	***Liabilities + Owner's Equity***		$61,370

FIGURE 11.13. Retail store Balance Sheet prepared from the Trial Balance Worksheet in Figure 11.8.

An account called "Cost of Goods Sold" is now added to your General Ledger and Trial Balance Worksheet (see Figure 11.14). The Inventory balance in your General Ledger Balance column on the worksheet is your beginning inventory. Debit (add) this figure to Cost of Goods Sold and credit (subtract) it from Inventory (see General Journal entry in Figure 11.15). Next, debit the amount in Purchases, Manufacturing Labor Expense, and Manufacturing Overhead to Cost of Goods Sold, and credit these amounts to the individual accounts (Figure 11.16). Finally, take the dollar value of your costed physical inventory at year end (see Chapter 13), credit (subtract) this amount from Cost of Goods Sold, and debit (add) it to Inventory (Figure 11.17).

As illustrated in Figure 11.14, after these adjustments are made, the Adjusted Trial Balance columns on your worksheet will show a new ending Inventory figure and Cost of Goods Sold figure. Purchases, Manufacturing Labor, and Manufacturing Overhead are now cleared (balance = 0) because they are part of Cost of Goods Sold. When transferring figures to your Income Statement, you should show how this Cost of Goods Sold figure was obtained, as illustrated in Figure 11.18. The end-of-year Inventory figure will appear as an asset on your Balance Sheet, as illustrated in Figure 11.19.

CLOSING OUT INCOME STATEMENT ACCOUNTS

Income Statement accounts must be closed out (balance = 0) at the end of each accounting period, which will generally be one year. These accounts record the revenues and expenses of a single accounting period and therefore must begin each new period with zero balances. Balance Sheet accounts, on the other hand, continue for the life of the business. Assets are increased and decreased; liabilities are incurred and paid up; owner's equity increases or decreases—all on a continuous basis.

The Income Statement shows *how* the owner's equity was increased (a profit made) or decreased (a loss incurred) in a particular period of time. By making the *opposite* entry for the debit or credit balance in each Revenue, Cost of Goods Sold, Owner's Withdrawal, and Expense account—and a matching (debit for credit, credit for debit) entry in the Owner's Equity Retained Earnings Account—you'll end up with zero balances in the Revenue, Cost of Goods Sold, Owner's Withdrawal, and Expense accounts. In addition, you'll have added (credited) the Net Earnings minus Owner's Withdrawal to Retained Earnings (note that if Net Earnings were less than Owner's Withdrawal, you'll have debited Retained Earnings with the difference).

In your General Journal you should make a clearing entry for all Income

XYZ

TRIAL BALANCE

	General Ledger Balance		Adjustments		Adjusted
	Debit	Credit	Debit	Credit	Debit
Cash	30000				30000
Accounts Rec.	20000				20000
Inventory	32000		30000 (7)	32000 (3)	30000
Fixed Assets	90000				90000
Accum. Dep.		34000		9500 (2)	
Accounts Payable		6000			
Loans Payable		35000			
Salaries Payable				800 (1)	
Owner's Capital		45000			
Retained Earnings		30500			
Sales		160000			
Discounts	2500				2500
Cost of Goods Sold			32000 (3)	30000 (7)	
			60000 (4)		
			5000 (5)		
			27600 (6)		94600
Purchases Ex.	60000			60000 (4)	
Mfg. Overhead Ex.	5000			5000 (5)	
Mfg. Labor Ex.	27000		600 (1)	27600 (6)	
Sales & Admin. Labor	22000		200 (1)		22200
Sales & Admin. Overhead	3000				3000
Advertising Ex.	2500				2500
Depreciation Ex.			9500 (2)		9500
Bad Debts Ex.	700				700
Misc. Ex.	800				800
Owner's Withdrawal	15000				15000
	310500	310500	164900	164900	320800

FIGURE 11.14. Trial Balance Worksheet for a manufacturing concern.

Manufacturing Company

As of 12/31/78

Trial Balance	Income Statement		Balance Sheet		
Credit	Debit	Credit	Debit	Credit	
			30000		
			20000		
			30000		
			90000		
43500				43500	
6000				6000	
35000				35000	
800				800	
45000				45000	
30500				30500	+ 9200 = 39,700
160000		160000			
	2500				
	94600				
	22200				
	3000				
	2500				
	9500				
	700				
	800				
	15000				
320800	150800	160000	170000	170000	
		150800			
		9200			

FIGURE 11.14. (Continued.)

GENERAL JOURNAL — Page 2

date		Description	debit	credit
12	31	Cost of Goods Sold	32000	
		Inventory		32000
		Add Beginning Inventory		
		to Cost of Goods Sold		

FIGURE 11.15. General Journal entry to transfer beginning inventory to cost of goods sold.

GENERAL JOURNAL — Page 2

date		description	debit	credit
12	31	Cost of Goods Sold	60000	
		Purchases Expense		60000
		Add purchases Expense to		
		Cost of Goods Sold		
		Cost of Goods Sold	5000	
		Mfg. Overhead Expense		5000
		Add Mfg. Overhead to		
		Cost of Goods Sold		
		Cost of Goods Sold	27600	
		Mfg. Labor Expense		27600
		Add Mfg. Labor Ex. to		
		Cost of goods sold		

FIGURE 11.16. General Journal entries to transfer purchases, manufacturing overhead, and manufacturing labor to cost of goods sold.

GENERAL JOURNAL Page____

	date		description	① debit	② credit
1	12	31	Inventory	30000	
2			Cost of Goods Sold		30000
3			Subtract Ending Inventory		
4			from Cost of Goods Sold		
5					
6					
7					
8					

FIGURE 11.17. General Journal entry to make the Inventory account show the year-end inventory and to subtract this inventory from the cost of goods sold.

XYZ MANUFACTURING COMPANY

INCOME STATEMENT FOR 1/1/95 TO 12/31/95

Gross Sales	$160,000	
less Discounts	(2,500)	
Net Sales		$157,500
Cost of Goods Sold		
Beginning Inventory	32,000	
plus Purchases	60,000	
plus Manufacturing Overhead	5,000	
plus Manufacturing Labor	27,600	
less Ending Inventory	(30,000)	
Cost of Goods Sold		94,600
Gross Profit		62,900
Sales & Administrative Expenses		
Salaries	22,200	
Overhead	3,000	
Advertising	2,500	
Depreciation Expense	9,500	
Bad Debts Expense	700	
Miscellaneous Expense	800	
Total Sales and Administrative Expenses		38,700
Net Earnings		24,200
Less Owner's Withdrawal		15,000
Earnings after Owner's Withdrawal		$ 9,200
Retained Earnings, Beginning of Year		30,500
Retained Earnings, End of Year		$ 39,700

FIGURE 11.18. Manufacturing Income Statement prepared from the Trial Balance Worksheet in Figure 11.14.

XYZ MANUFACTURING COMPANY
BALANCE SHEET AS OF 12/31/95

Assets			*Liabilities*			
Cash		$ 30,000	Accounts Payable			$ 6,000
Accounts Receivable		20,000	Loans Payable			35,000
Inventory		30,000	Salaries Payable			800
			Total Liabilities			41,800
Fixed Assets	90,000					
Less Accumulated			*Owner's Equity*			
Depreciation	43,500		Owner's Capital		45,000	
Total Fixed Assets		46,500	Retained Earnings		39,700	
			Total Owner's Equity			84,700
Total Assets		$126,500	*Owner's Equity + Liabilities*			$126,500

FIGURE 11.19. Manufacturing Balance Sheet prepared from the Trial Balance Worksheet in Figure 11.14.

Statement accounts as illustrated in Figure 11.20. These entries were made from the Trial Balance Worksheet in Figure 11.8. When they are posted to the General Ledger accounts, the balances will be zero (see Figure 11.21). Note that the last entry in the General Journal in Figure 11.20 shows the addition of Retained Earnings from the Income Statement to the Retained Earnings account. Now the debit and credit clearing entries will balance. The new credit balance in the Retained Earnings account should appear on your Balance Sheet.

With all Income Statement account balances at zero, and Balance Sheet accounts for Retained Earnings and Inventory showing new end-of-the-year balances, you're ready to start recording next year's transactions—once you reverse any accruals.

REVERSING PRIOR YEAR'S ACCRUALS

Accruals are adjustments made for actual or estimated expenses applicable to one accounting period but actually paid in the following period. By recording an accrued expense at 12/31/95, you are *recognizing* that expense for accounting purposes in 1995. You will actually pay the expense in 1996,

GENERAL JOURNAL Page 4

	date	description	① debit	② credit
1	1/1	Sales	900 00	
2		Cost of Goods Sold		525 00
3		Misc. Revenues	6 00	
4		Payroll Expense		152 00
5		Rent Expense		24 00
6		Advertising Expense		15 00
7		Sales Tax Expense		10 80
8		Depreciation Expense		13 00
9		Misc. Expense		4 00
10		Owner's Withdrawal		60 00
11		Retained Earnings		102 20
12		To Clear Income	906 00	906 00
13		Statement Accounts		
14				
15				

FIGURE 11.20. General Journal entries made to close out Income Statement accounts at the beginning of the new year. These figures were taken from the Trial Balance Worksheet in Figure 11.8.

PAYROLL EXPENSE

1995 date	items	folio	debits	1995 date	items	folio	credits
1-31	Jan. Payroll	CD-1	600 -	8-15	Tax Payment Refund	CR-8	15 -
2-29	Feb. "	CD-2	650 -				
3-31	March "	CD-2	600 -				
4-30	April "	CD-3	650 -				
5-31	May "	CD-4	640 -				
6-30	June "	CD-5	630 -				
7-31	July "	CD-5	600 -				
8-31	Aug. "	CD-6	650 -				
9-30	Sept. "	CD-6	640 -				
10-31	Oct. "	CD-7	620 -				
11-30	Nov. "	CD-8	650 -				
12-31	Dec. "	CD-9	630 -				
12-31	Accrued Payroll Expense	GJ-2	60				
	* 7605		7620 -				15 -
	** -0-			12-31	To Clear Account	GJ-4	7605 -
							7620 -
1996				1996			
1-31	Jan. Payroll	CD-10	640 -	1-1	Reverse Accrued Payroll	GJ-5	*** 60 -

* This is the December 31, 1995 balance used on the financial statements.

** The balance is zero after the entry is made to clear the account.

*** The corresponding entry for this adjustment is a debit to accrued payroll expense.

FIGURE 11.21. Example illustrating how a clearing entry closes out Income Statement accounts. After the clearing entry of $7,605, the balance equals zero. Note that the Accrued Payroll Expense of 12/31 is reversed by a credit entry of $60 on January 1. Then the January Payroll is listed as usual at the end of January. You will probably start a new page for a new year, but this illustrates what happens from one year to the next.

but do not want your 1996 financial statements to also reflect the expense. This is why you will record an entry to reverse the prior year's accruals.

Figure 11.21 illustrates the reversal of a year-end payroll expense accrual.

MONTHLY FINANCIAL STATEMENTS

Depending on the size and activity of your business, you may wish to prepare financial statements on a monthly rather than on only a yearly basis. The most useful statement to have on a monthly basis is the Income Statement, and you can prepare it monthly without making all the end-of-the-year adjustments discussed above. Inventory can be estimated or taken from perpetual inventory records.

Monthly financial statements should be prepared from the Trial Balance Worksheet. Accruals should only be made on the worksheet—not in the General Journal and General Ledger. You will also *not* close out income statement accounts or record reversing entries on a monthly basis. This is only done at the end of your accounting year.

INCOME TAXES

Single proprietorships and partnerships are not subject to federal income taxes and normally are not required to pay state income taxes (check with your accountant or state income tax department to find out if this is true in your state). The net profit or loss from proprietorships is computed on a Schedule C, Profit or Loss from Business or Profession, and added to other personal income on Form 1040, U.S. Individual Income Tax Return. The information from your Trial Balance Worksheet is used to fill out Schedule C. The IRS Publication 334, *Tax Guide for Small Businesses* is helpful in filling

XYZ MANUFACTURING CORPORATION
INCOME STATEMENT FOR 1/1/95 TO 12/31/95

Sales		$500,000
Cost of Goods Sold		354,700
Gross Profit		145,300
Operating Expenses		
Selling	41,800	
General & Administrative	83,400	
Total Operating Expenses		125,200
Income from Operations		20,100
Other Income		
Gain on Sale of Machinery		5,700
Earnings before Income Taxes		25,800
Income Taxes		11,100
Net Earnings		$ 14,700
Retained Earnings		
Beginning of year		13,800
End of year		$ 28,500
Net earnings per share (based on 10,000 shares outstanding)		$1.47

FIGURE 11.22. Corporation Income Statement.

XYZ MANUFACTURING CORPORATION
BALANCE SHEET AS OF 12/31/95

Current Assets		
Cash		$ 40,000
Accounts Receivable, less allowance for doubtful accounts of $1,500		32,500
Inventories:		
Raw Materials	20,000	
Work in Process	5,000	
Finished Goods	35,000	
Total Inventories		60,000
Prepaid Expenses		3,900
Deposits		4,000
Advance to Supplier		3,500
Total Current Assets		143,900
Property, Plant & Equipment		
Land	10,000	
Building	45,000	
Machinery & Equipment	35,000	
	90,000	
Less Accumulated Depreciation	26,900	
		63,100
Total Assets		$207,000

Current Liabilities		
Note Payable to Bank		$ 20,000
Accounts Payable		26,000
Salaries Payable		7,000
Payroll Taxes Payable		4,500
Income Taxes Payable		6,100
Total Current Liabilities		63,600
Long-Term Note Payable		14,900
Stockholder's Equity		
Common Stock, par value $10.00 per share, issued and outstanding, 10,000 shares	100,000	
Retained Earnings	28,500	
Total Stockholder's Equity		128,500
Liabilities and Stockholder's Equity		$207,000

FIGURE 11.23. Corporation Balance Sheet.

out Schedule C. This booklet also contains information for filing partnership returns.

Corporations, on the other hand, are subject to federal, and in most cases, state income taxes on earnings. These will be deducted from Income to get Net Income, as illustrated in the Corporate Income Statement in Figure 11.22. Figure 11.23 shows a Corporate Balance Sheet.

As discussd in Chapter 2, subchapter S corporations are not subject to federal income taxes. They are taxed in certain states, however.

SUMMING UP

The Trial Balance Worksheet is your basic tool for checking the accuracy of General Ledger account balances, making end-of-the-year adjustments, and preparing financial statements. When Retained Earnings for the year have been computed by subtracting Owner's Withdrawal from Net Earnings on the Income Statement, add (credit) this amount to your Balance Sheet Retained Earnings account and clear (balance = 0) your General Ledger Income Statement accounts. If you suffered a loss, the amount should be subtracted (debited) from Retained Earnings. After reversing accruals (if any), you'll be ready to start recording the following year's transactions.

12

Retail Store Accounting

If you operate a retail store, there are two areas you should maintain careful control over: (1) daily sales transactions, and (2) inventories. Cash comes into your business every day in the form of bills, coins, checks, and credit card receipts. You need to know exactly how much comes in every day and in what form, so that you can accurately record sales and cash receipts.

Inventories are another critical aspect of running a retail store. You need to know what is paid for goods in order to know what to charge for them, and to ascertain whether or not you made a profit from selling them. The method you use to value your inventory will also affect how much profit or loss you record at the end of the year.

CONTROLLING CASH AND SALES

It's particulary important in a retail store to keep a record of all sales transactions and to maintain control over all cash flowing in and out of your cash register or cash box.

Sales Slips. For each sale which takes place, a pre-numbered sales slip should be completed listing the specific details of the sale, including a description of the item sold, the price, sales tax, discounts allowed, and the method of payment. Recording details of the sale serves two purposes: (1) the customer will have a record of the purchase; and (2) you'll have information needed to help control your inventory. By using pre-numbered sales slips and accounting for consecutive numbers at the end of each day, you can insure that all sales have been recorded.

Cash Registers. Cash registers vary widely in sophistication, from those which merely record the amount of a sale to those which keep detailed records of the means of payment as well as automatically updating inventory records for the items which have been sold. The benefit of a cash register is that it provides a record of all sales made during the day for double checking against the day's receipts. It's often appropriate, but not always necessary, to use sales slips as well as a cash register for controlling sales and cash.

An alternative to using a cash register is a cash drawer. In this case, cash and credit card receipts may be kept in a locked drawer for security between transactions. It's important, however, to ensure that pre-numbered sales slips are completed for each sale in order to provide details of the day's sales for cash balancing, reordering and inventory-keeping purposes.

Change Fund. A change fund is a fixed amount of cash kept in the cash register or cash drawer for making change. At the end of each day, this amount will be left in the cash drawer (or in a safe if you keep a large change fund) and the day's receipts will be deposited in the bank.

KINDS OF SALES

Cash Sales. This includes sales paid for with cash, customer checks or bank credit cards such as Master Card or American Express. In the case of credit card sales, the full amount of the sale should be recorded, and any fee payable to the credit card companies should be recorded as an expense when it is charged to your account.

Charge Sales. These are sales for which you bill your customers on charge accounts.

Layaway Sales. Layaway sales are when customers leave a deposit on merchandise which is set aside for them. When the initial payment is made, a cash sale should be recorded and a layaway receivable set up for the amount still due. As payments are made, the receivable is reduced.

OTHER ITEMS RELATED TO SALES

Sales Taxes. Sales tax on cash and charge sales should be itemized on cash register tapes and sales slips. The amount of sales tax should be included in sales totals. When you make payments of totals accumulated from register tapes or sales slips, you will reduce sales by the amount paid.

Discounts. If you allow discounts to employees or other customers, these amounts should be deducted from the total amount of the sale.

Returns and Refunds. Refunds given to customers should be recorded as reductions of sales.

Voids. Occasionally a sale may be incorrectly recorded on the cash register. If possible, the register should be entered for a negative amount equal to the amount of the incorrect entry. If not, keep a careful record for cash balancing purposes.

CASH BALANCING/DAILY SUMMARY

At the end of each day, it's important to tally the total amount of sales recorded by the cash register and/or pre-numbered sales slips (all sales slip numbers used during the day must be accounted for) and to reconcile this amount to the cash on hand. If you have more than one cash register, separate daily summaries should be prepared. Then the totals can be combined before posting to the Cash Receipts Journal. Figure 12.1 illustrates a typical daily summary.

Item 1: The total of the day's cash sales.

Item 2: Represents cash collected on prior days' charge sales.

Item 3: The total amount of cash that must be accounted for.

Item 4: This will be the total of all cash, checks and bank credit card slips in the cash register at the end of the day.

Item 5: The balance in your change fund—the money you had in the register at the beginning of the day and will leave there for the next day.

Item 6: The amount you will deposit in the bank. It should agree with item 7, "total receipts to be accounted for".

Item 7: The same as item 3.

Item 8: If item 7 is greater than item 6, you have a shortage. This could be caused by an error in recording a sale, giving a customer too much change, or taking money out of the cash register or cash drawer without recording it. Shortages should be recorded as an expense.

Item 9: If item 7 is less than item 6, you have a cash overage. This could be caused by neglecting to record a sale, recording a sale for the wrong amount, or giving a customer too little change. Overages should be recorded as an offset to shortages (in the same General Ledger account).

DAILY SUMMARY

Cash Receipts

1. Cash sales		$325.00
2. Collections on account		100.00
3. Total receipts to be accounted for		$425.00

Cash on Hand

4. Cash in register:		
Coins	24.00	
Bills	310.00	
Checks	57.00	
Bank credit card slips	80.00	
Total cash in register		471.00
5. Less change fund		50.00
6. Total cash deposit		421.00
7. Total receipts to be accounted for (Item 3)		425.00
8. Cash short (Item 7 greater than Item 6)		4.00
9. Cash over (Item 7 less than Item 6)		----

Total Sales

10. Cash sales		325.00
11. Charge sales		250.00
12. Total sales		$575.00

FIGURE 12.1. Daily summary of sales and cash transactions for a retail store.

Item 10: Same as item 1.

Item 11: Sales made on customers' charge accounts with your store.

Item 12: The total of all sales made that day.

RECORDING DAILY SUMMARY TOTALS IN CASH RECEIPTS JOURNAL

Cash and sales transactions should be recorded in the Cash Receipts Journal from the daily summaries. Figure 12.2 illustrates how the transactions summarized in Figure 12.1 would be recorded in the Cash Receipts Journal:

CASH RECEIPTS JOURNAL

		1	2	3	4	5	6	
	date	amount	Sales	Accounts Receivable	Overage (Shortage)	general account	general amount	
1	6-1	421-	575-	(150-)	(4)			1
2								2
3								3
4								4
5								5
6								6
7								7
8								8
9								9
10								10
11								11
12								12
13								13
14								14
15								15
16								16
17								17
18								18
19								19
20								20
21								21
22								22
23								23
24								24
25								25

FIGURE 12.2. Posting of cash and sales transactions in the Cash Receipts Journal from the daily summary.

Amount. This is the total cash deposited in the bank. It's the amount of Item 6. When posted to the General Ledger, this will be a debit to Cash.

Sales. This represents the total of both cash and charge sales. It's from Item 12 on the daily summary. When posted to the General Ledger, this will be a credit to Sales.

Accounts Receivable. This is total charge sales from Item 11, less collections on account from Item 2. Since there were more charge sales than collections on account, accounts receivable should be increased in the General Ledger by debiting the account. This is why the amount is in brackets in Figure 12.2. Generally, all items in the Cash Receipts Journal except for cash will be a credit in the General Ledger. If they are debits, the amounts should be bracketed in the Cash Receipts Journal.

Overage/(Shortage). This is the amount from Item 8. Overages will be credited to the General Ledger account, and shortages will be debited. When you prepare financial statements, a net debit balance in this account will be a miscellaneous expense item and a net credit balance will be a reduction of miscellaneous expenses.

INVENTORY AND COST OF GOODS SOLD

Inventories are stocks of merchandise on hand available for sale. In a retail store it's important to know what you have in stock, how fast it's moving, and when to reorder. You'll also need to place a dollar value on your inventory at least once a year for income tax purposes. The two major concerns in connection with inventories are: what are the quantities on hand, and what is the dollar value of the inventory.

Inventory Quantities. In some small shops you can estimate inventory quantities for reorder purposes by merely checking your shelves visually. However, a perpetual inventory system may be necessary, at least for some inventory items. Figure 12.3 illustrates a typical perpetual inventory sheet for a single product.

Note that the perpetual inventory sheet has a place to record sales of the merchandise, shipments received, and the balance in stock. Columns are also provided to list goods ordered and the price paid for them.

Perpetual inventory records are useful for reorder decisions. They indicate how fast an item is moving, time lapse between order placement and receipt of goods, and prices paid. You can also use quantities from perpetual records as a basis for calculating the dollar value of inventories for financial statement and income tax purposes. At least once a year, however, a physical

PERPETUAL INVENTORY RECORD

Product Name ______ Code ______ Page 1

date	unit sales	units on order	shipments rec'd	price	balance in stock
1/15		150		2 ea.	0
2/10			150	300	150
3/1	35				115
4/1	60				55
4/2		200		2.10 ea	55
5/1	45				10
5/3			200		210

FIGURE 12.3. Perpetual inventory record. Set it up to give the necessary information needed to make re-order decisions. Periodically (at least once a year) match perpetual inventory balance with a physical inventory.

inventory should be taken to determine inventory quantities. By matching your physical and perpetual inventory records, you'll find errors in your perpetual records, indications of theft, and other losses.

Valuation of Inventories. Determining the dollar value of inventories is one of the most difficult, and most important, accounting functions for a retailer. We won't go into all of the complexities of inventory pricing, but give simple illustrations of some of the methods available. We suggest that you seek help from your accountant or tax specialist when you value your inventories.

Pricing Inventory Quantities. Once you have a reliable tally of all merchandise item quantities; either from a physical count or from perpetual records, you must place a value on each item. This value should be the cost of the item.

The most accurate way to value inventory is to keep a record of the cost of every item in stock. The total value of your inventory would then be the total of all those costs. Unless your business has a small inventory of high value items, (such as a jewelery store would, for example) it may be impractical to identify the specific cost of every item on hand. The first-in, first-out (FIFO) and last-in, first-out (LIFO) methods of determining inventory cost can be used where specific costs aren't known. These inventory costing methods are described in Chapter 13.

Since most retail stores carry a diversity of products which are acquired at different prices on different dates, it's often impractical to determine cost on the LIFO or FIFO methods. Because of this, retailers have developed special methods of estimating the cost of their inventories. These are the Gross Margin Method and the Retail Method.

Gross Margin Method of Estimating Inventory Cost. The gross margin method of estimating inventory cost can be used if you have a standard (or average) gross margin that is applied to your total inventory or groups of merchandise.

Since merchandise in a store is generally marked with retail prices, you can obtain the retail value of your merchandise by merely adding up those prices. This is much easier than looking up the cost of each item.

Once you have a total inventory based on retail price, the cost can be estimated by applying the gross margin percentage. For example, if your merchandise cost is generally 60% of the retail selling price, your gross margin percentage is 40%. Assuming the retail value of your inventory is $20,000, the estimated cost is calculated as follows:

$20,000 × 40% = $8,000 (gross margin)

	$20,000	- inventory at retail
minus	8,000	- gross margin
	$12,000	- estimated cost

If your gross margin varies from one department to another, you should take separate inventory totals for each department and then apply the various gross margins to arrive at estimated cost.

You can use the gross margin method to estimate your inventory value without physically counting your merchandise. To use this method you must know the cost of your beginning inventory, purchases at cost, and sales at retail.

The calculation works as follows:

Beginning inventory at cost	$ 40,000
Purchases during the period at cost	120,000
Merchandise available for sale	$160,000

Less Cost of Goods Sold:

Sales at retail	$110,000	
Gross margin percentage	40%	
Gross margin (40% × 110,000) = $44,000		
Cost of goods sold (110,000 − 44,000) =		$ 66,000
Inventory at cost		$ 94,000

Retail Method of Estimating Inventory Cost. This method of estimating inventory cost is similar to the gross margin method, except that you must keep track of both the cost and retail value of purchases. It works as follows:

	COST	*RETAIL*
Inventory at beginning of period	$ 5,000	$ 7,500
Purchases during the period	55,000	92,500
Totals	60,000	100,000

$$\text{Ratio of cost to retail} = \frac{60{,}000}{100{,}000} = 60\%$$

Sales for period	90,000
Inventory at retail ($100,000 – $90,000)	$ 10,000

Inventory computation — 60% of $10,000 = $6,000 estimated inventory at cost.

Cost of Goods Sold. Once you know the dollar value of your inventory, you can determine cost of goods sold. Cost of goods sold is arrived at by adding beginning inventory (what you started with at the beginning of the period) to purchases, and subtracting ending inventory. In the example

INCOME STATEMENT FROM 1/1/96 TO 12/31/96

Sales		$160,000
Cost of Goods Sold		
Beginning Inventory	20,000	
Plus Purchases	120,000	
Goods Available for Sale	140,000	
Less Ending Inventory	25,000	
Cost of Goods Sold		115,000
Gross Profit		45,000
Operating Expenses		
Salaries	12,000	
Rent	3,600	
Utilities	900	
Advertising	3,500	
Insurance	500	
Miscellaneous	500	
Total Operating Expenses		21,000
Net Earnings		$ 24,000

FIGURE 12.4. Income Statement for a retail store. Cost of goods sold is computed by adding purchases to beginning inventory and subtracting ending inventory.

shown in Figure 12.4 the dollar value of inventory at 1/1/95 was $20,000. During 1996 you purchased $120,000 worth of goods. Total goods available for sale during the year totaled $140,000. Since the value of the inventory at the end of the year (12/31/96) was $25,000, cost of goods sold was $115,000.

Be careful when valuing your inventory, since inventory value has a direct effect on your profit or loss. Looking again at Figure 12.4, notice that if you value your ending inventory high, it will increase your gross profits for the year and decrease them the following year (this year's ending inventory becomes next year's beginning inventory); and, vice versa, if you undervalue your ending inventory, it will decrease this year's gross profits and increase next year's.

SUMMING UP

In order to maintain control over cash and sales, summarize each day's transactions on a daily summary. Use the tallies on your summary sheet to reconcile the sales recorded by cash register (or pre-numbered sales slips) to the cash on hand. If you have more than one cash register, prepare separate daily summaries and combine them before posting to the Cash Receipts Journal.

Keep track of inventory quantities by recording sales, shipments received, etc., on a perpetual inventory sheet. (In some small shops, it may be possible to *estimate* inventory quantities by checking your shelves visually.) At least once a year, take a physical inventory and match it against your perpetual records, correcting any discrepancies which arise.

To value your inventory, choose a method given in this chapter, or ask an accountant or tax specialist for advice on the best method for your business. Once you have valued your inventory, compute the cost of goods sold by adding beginning inventory to purchases, and subtracting ending inventory. Remember that the value of your inventory will have a direct effect on your profit or loss.

13

Accounting For Manufacturing Expenses

As a manufacturer, you'll want to separate your manufacturing expenses from your sales and administrative expenses. This is necessary in order for you to calculate the cost of making your products, that is, the cost of goods sold. You'll also have to keep track of an inventory, which will be made up at any one time of raw materials, work in process, and finished goods. In this chapter we'll discuss how to record your manufacturing expenses, compute the cost of goods sold, place a value on your physical inventory, and keep a perpetual inventory record.

INCOME STATEMENT

A sample income statement for a manufacturing company is shown in Figure 13.1. Note that the cost of goods sold is arrived at by adding the beginning inventory (the inventory at the beginning of the year) to purchases, labor, and manufacturing overhead, and subtracting the ending inventory. Purchases include all raw materials used to manufacture the products. Labor is the direct labor costs (salaries to employees who make the products; not salespeople, clerical help, etc.) including salaries, payroll taxes, and benefits. Manufacturing overhead is a percentage of total rent, utilities, etc., which is allocated to the manufacturing end of the business. For example, if five-sixths of your building is used for manufacturing and one-sixth for office space, you would allocate five-sixths of your rent expense to manufacturing overhead.

LABOR COSTS

In order to separate manufacturing labor costs from sales and administrative labor costs, you should maintain separate salary expense accounts in your

INCOME STATEMENT FROM 1/1/96 TO 12/31/96

Sales		$300,000
Cost of Goods Sold		
Beginning Inventory	50,000	
Purchases	75,000	
Labor	125,000	
Manufacturing Overhead	25,000	
	275,000	
Less Ending Inventory	75,000	
Cost of Goods Sold		200,000
Gross Profit		100,000
Sales and Administrative Expenses		
Salaries	30,000	
Rent	2,500	
Utilities	500	
Office Supplies	300	
Printing Supplies	1,000	
Promotion Expenses	15,000	
Insurance	500	
Miscellaneous	200	
Sales and Administrative Expenses		50,000
Net Earnings		$ 50,000

FIGURE 13.1. Income Statement for a manufacturing company showing how cost of goods sold is figured.

General Ledger as shown in Figure 13.2. Salaries for sales people, office clerks, etc., would be posted to sales and administrative salaries expenses. Salaries for laborers, foremen, and manufacturing supervisors would be posted to manufacturing labor expenses. If you have a large number of employees, you may wish to have two columns in your Cash Disbursements Journal for listing salary expenses, as shown in Figure 13.3.

If you have an employee whose time is divided between manufacturing and administrative or sales functions (for example, a general manager), you can handle the division in either of two ways. If you have a general manager who devotes 40 percent of his or her time to manufacturing and 60 percent to

MANUFACTURING SALARIES EXPENSE

DATE 19__	ITEMS	FOLIO	√	DEBITS	DATE 19__	ITEMS	FOLIO	√	CREDITS
3 31	March Salaries	CD-5		1512 –					

SALES & ADMINISTRATIVE SALARIES EXPENSE

DATE 19__	ITEMS	FOLIO	√	DEBITS	DATE 19__	ITEMS	FOLIO	√	CREDITS
3 31	March Salaries	CD-5		824					

FIGURE 13.2. Separate labor expenses by keeping a separate account for manufacturing salaries and one for sales and administrative salaries, as shown here.

CASH DISBURSEMENTS JOURNAL — Page 5

	date	payee	① check#	② total	③ mfg.sal.	④ Ad.sal	⑤ raw material	⑥ mfg. suppls.	⑦ general	⑧ gen. acct name
1	3 1	M. Smith	4052	225-	225-					
2		R. Boland	4053	210-	210-					
3		S. Leland	4054	320-	170-	150-				
4		R. Beecher	4055	180-		180-				
5										
6										
7										
8										
9										
10										
11										
12										
13										
14										
15										
16										
17										
18										
19										
20										

FIGURE 13.3. Example of separate columns in Cash Disbursements Journal for manufacturing salaries and sales and administrative salaries.

administration and sales, you could list the manager's whole salary under administration and sales expenses. Then at the end of the year when you prepare to make up financial statements, credit sales and administrative salary expenses with 40 percent of the manager's yearly salary and debit manufacturing labor expenses with the same amount. Another solution would be to allocate 40 percent of this salary to manufacturing expenses throughout the year.

MANUFACTURING OVERHEAD

Throughout the year, keep track of rent, utilities, insurance, supplies, etc., in the usual manner. Then before preparing your financial statements, decide what percentage of these costs should be allocated to manufacturing overhead. You may base this on the amount of space that's used for manufacturing, or use some other method that you feel more accurately reflects the overhead used. For example, if there are two toilets in the plant and one in the office, you can allocate two-thirds of the cost of toilet supplies to manufacturing overhead. Or you may wish to come up with one fraction or percentage to apply to the total amount of overhead expenses.

PURCHASES

Your purchases of raw materials and the supplies used in manufacturing are recorded separately from purchases for administrative or other uses. Chapter 5 shows several methods for recording purchases depending on whether you're on a cash or accrual basis of accounting. Since you're a manufacturer, you'll want to use either method 2 or 3. You must keep separate accounts in your General Ledger for manufacturing purchases and administrative and sales purchases.

INVENTORY

At least once a year you must determine the dollar value of your inventory for income tax and financial statement purposes. In order to do this you must take a physical count to determine how much of each item you have on hand and then place a dollar value on each item.

In a manufacturing company the physical inventory at any one time usually consists of some finished goods, some work in process, and some raw materials. When you take your physical inventory, you should separate it into these three categories. You'll then be ready to cost (compute) the value of this inventory.

Inventory Cost. Your inventory should be valued at cost (what you paid for it). If you could match each inventory item with its invoice, you could use the specific cost method. You generally can't identify each item's specific cost, however, since you'll be constantly buying and using the same kinds of items. You must, therefore, make an assumption to determine which items remain in inventory and which were sold. You can use either the first-in, first-out (FIFO), or last-in, first-out (LIFO) methods to identify cost.

The FIFO method assumes that the items you purchased or produced first are the first items you sold (although they may not, in fact, be the first ones you sold). The items in inventory at the end of the year are valued as the items most recently purchased or produced.

The LIFO method assumes that the items of inventory that you purchased last are the ones you sold first. Thus, items included in your ending inventory are considered to be those from the opening inventory plus those items acquired in the earlier part of the year.

The FIFO and LIFO methods will produce different results in income depending on the trend of price levels of the goods in inventory. In times of inflation when prices are rising, LIFO will produce a larger cost of goods sold and a lower closing inventory. Under FIFO, the cost of goods sold will be lower and the closing inventory will be higher. However, in times of falling prices, LIFO will produce a smaller cost of goods sold and a higher inventory. Under FIFO, the reverse is true.

The following example shows the contrasting results of figuring the cost of goods sold under the LIFO and FIFO methods. Because of the complex Internal Revenue Service rules involving the use of the LIFO method which are not discussed here, we suggest that you consult your accountant or tax specialist before deciding to use it.

EXAMPLE. In the tax year 1990 you have an opening inventory of 1,000 units of an item. Your inventory is made up of 500 units purchased in 1988 at $1.00 a unit and 500 units purchased in 1989 at $1.50 a unit.

In 1990 you purchased an additional 500 units: 200 units at $2.00 a unit in February and 300 units at $3.00 a unit in July.

By the close of the tax year 1990, you sold 1,250 units leaving a closing inventory of 250 units.

COST OF GOODS SOLD UNDER FIFO

Opening inventory		
500 units @ $1.00	$500	
500 units @ $1.50	750	$1,250
Plus:		
Goods purchased during the year		
200 units @ $2.00	$400	
300 units @ $3.00	900	1,300
Cost of goods available for sale		$2,550
Minus:		
Closing inventory (1,500 less 1,250 = 250) 250 units @ $3.00 (the last 250 units purchased remaining in inventory)		750
Cost of goods sold		$1,800

COST OF GOODS SOLD UNDER LIFO

Opening inventory (adjusted to average cost) 1000 units @ $1.25		$1,250.00
Plus:		
Goods purchased during year		
200 units @ $2.00	$400.00	
300 units @ $3.00	900.00	1,300.00
Cost of goods available for sale		$2,550.00
Minus:		
Closing inventory 250 units (units of opening inventory remain in inventory) $1.25 (average cost per unit)		312.50
Cost of goods sold		$2,237.50

Lower of Cost or Market. If you use the FIFO method of determining cost, you can value your inventory at either cost, or the lower of cost or market. Lower of cost or market means that you compare the market value of each item on hand at the inventory date with its cost and use the lower value as its inventory value. Thus, if at the end of your tax year you had the following items on hand, the value of your closing inventory would be $600.

Items	*Cost*	*Market*	*Whichever is lower*
R	$300	$500	$300
S	200	100	100
T	450	200	200
Totals	$950	$800	$600

If you use this method, you must value each item in the inventory. You may not value the entire inventory at cost ($950) and at market ($800) and use the lower of the two figures. If you use the cost basis, the value of your closing inventory would be $950.

You cannot use the lower of cost or market method if you use the LIFO method to cost your inventory.

Due to the complexity of the LIFO method, the following examples will use the FIFO method to determine cost.

Raw Materials. Your first step in computing the value of your ending inventory is to cost all raw materials in stock using the FIFO method.

Finished Goods. Finished goods should be valued at what it costs you to make them, unless their market value is lower than this figure, as it might be for obsolete goods or products that have gone out of style and will have to be sold at a loss. In this instance, use the market value of the goods. Normally, however, you should value finished goods at what it costs you to make them. This means you have to compute the raw materials, labor, and manufacturing overhead expenses it costs to produce them.

You may have already established what it costs you to make your products. You may, for example, work on an overall gross margin for each product line. You know that you sell Product A for $40, leaving you a gross margin of $10, or 25 percent. If your average gross margin is 25 percent on all products, you could compute the value of finished goods by taking 75 percent of their total sale price.

Work in Process. To estimate the value of work in process, take a percentage of the finished goods value of the items. For example, if a finished Product A is worth $6.00, one that is half finished will be worth $3.00. The closer to completion, the closer to full value the work in process will be worth. A straight fraction may not always be accurate, however. Suppose $50 worth of raw materials were put into a product that was still only half finished in terms of labor. It would be worth $50 plus half the labor costs, plus half the overhead costs.

It's difficult to give any one method for valuing inventories in manufacturing firms because of the variations in each company. As a general guideline, the larger the ending inventory is in comparison to cost of goods sold, the more accurately it should be costed.

Looking again at Figure 13.1, you'll notice that the higher the value given to ending inventory, the higher the gross profit margin. If you overvalue the worth of your ending inventory, you'll show a higher profit that year and consequently a lower profit margin the following year (because the first year's ending inventory becomes the next year's beginning inventory); and, vice versa, if you undervalue your inventory, you'll show a lower profit the first year and a higher one the next year.

COSTING INVENTORY BY ESTIMATING VALUE OF FINISHED GOODS AND WORK IN PROCESS*

This method has been used successfully by small manufacturers to compute the value of their inventories. It's based on the ratio of total labor and overhead expenses to total materials to which labor has been applied. In addition, you must assign a completion factor (percentage) to work in process and have costed separately the materials in (1) raw materials, (2) work in process, and (3) finished goods inventories.

To cost your inventory using this method, do the following: *In first year of operations* (assuming no beginning inventory) you'll need the following figures from your end-of-the-year trial balance (see Chapter 11): total manufacturing labor expense; total manufacturing overhead expense; and total manufacturing purchases. For this example, we'll assume:

Total year manufacturing labor expense:	$100,000
Total year manufacturing overhead expense:	200,000
Total year manufacturing purchases:	700,000

* This method is not recommended if a product mix is not homogeneous, that is, if there's a wide variation in the proportion of materials, labor, and overhead costs of the products. For example, cloth and finished clothing are not homogeneous because there's a larger percentage of labor in the total cost of manufacturing finished clothing than cloth.

Use the FIFO method (see above) to cost your raw materials inventory. Using this same method, cost the *materials* in work in process and finished goods inventories. For our example, we'll assume:

Raw materials inventory:	\$ 60,000
Materials in work in process:	30,000
Materials in finished goods:	40,000
Total materials in inventory:	\$130,000

Adjust the total year purchases figure by subtracting your raw materials inventory:

\$700,000 − \$60,000 = \$640,000 adjusted purchases

This adjusted purchases figure more accurately reflects the value of all materials to which labor has been applied throughout the year. Add labor to overhead expenses and divide by adjusted purchases:

\$100,000 + \$200,000 = \$300,000 ÷ \$640,000 = .468 =
47 percent labor and overhead: purchases ratio

Next, estimate the average percentage completion of work in process. In other words, if work in process is spread out evenly—from one percent to 99 percent completed—you may want to use a 50 percent completion factor. If more goods are nearer to completion, you may feel 60 percent or 75 percent would be more accurate. In any case, pick one average percentage to use as your completion factor. In our example we'll use 75 percent.

To compute the labor and overhead costs of finished goods inventory, multiply the materials cost times the labor and overhead: purchases ratio:

\$40,000 × .47 = \$18,800 labor and overhead cost of finished goods

To compute the labor and overhead costs of work in process, first multiply by the completion factor (75 percent), then by the labor and overhead: purchases ratio:

\$30,000 × 75 percent × .47 =
\$10,575 labor and overhead cost of work in process

By adding these labor and overhead costs to total materials costs, you get the total cost of your inventory:

Total materials in inventory:	$130,000
Labor and overhead cost of finished goods:	18,800
Labor and overhead cost of work in process:	10,575
	$159,375 total inventory

The following is a chart illustrating the process:

	Col. 1	Col. 2	Col. 3	Col. 4	Col. 5	Col. 6
	Materials cost at FIFO	Completion factor	Col. 1 × Col. 2	Labor and overhead: purchases ratio	Col. 4 × Col. 3	Col. 1 + Col. 5
Raw materials	60,000	0	0	.47	0	60,000
Work in process	30,000	.75	22,500	.47	10,575	40,575
Finished goods	40,000	1.00	40,000	.47	18,800	58,800
Total	130,000		62,500		29,375	159,375

Note that no labor and overhead are assigned to the raw materials, with a completion factor of zero. Finished goods have a 100 percent completion factor.

For Second and Succeeding Years of Operation. You can't assume that the ratio of labor and overhead costs to purchases will remain the same from year to year. You may have improved the efficiency of your operation and therefore be using less labor or overhead, or both, for each dollar of purchases; or your product mix may be changed so that now you're producing items that use more labor or overhead costs, or both, per purchases dollar.

To adjust the purchases figure in the second year, add the beginning year's raw materials inventory and subtract the ending raw materials inventory. This will give you an adjusted purchases figure that accurately reflects the value of all materials to which labor has been applied throughout the year (beginning raw materials inventory must be added to purchases because these materials were used up during the year).

To begin, first price out (using FIFO) your raw materials and materials used in work in process and finished goods inventories, as you did the prior year. For our example, let's assume the following:

	Col. 1	Col. 2	Col. 3	Col. 4	Col. 5	Col. 6
	Materials cost at FIFO	Completion factor	Col. 1 × Col. 2	Labor and overhead: purchases ratio	Col. 4 × Col. 3	Col. 1 + Col. 5
Raw materials	70,000	0	0			
Work in process	35,000	.75	26,250			
Finished goods	50,000	1.00	50,000			
Total	155,000		76,250			

Note that the completion factor was the same as last year, although it may very well be different. From the trial balance, take the total manufacturing labor, overhead, and purchases figures as follows:

Total manufacturing labor:	$150,000
Total manufacturing overhead:	200,000
Total manufacturing purchases:	900,000

To adjust the purchases figure, add the beginning raw materials inventory and subtract the ending raw materials inventory as follows:

Purchases:	$900,000	
Plus raw materials, beginning inventory:	60,000	(last year's ending inventory)
	$960,000	
Less raw materials, ending inventory	70,000	
	$890,000	adjusted purchases

To compute labor and overhead: purchases ratio, add labor to overhead and divide by adjusted purchases as follows:

$$\$150{,}000 + \$200{,}000 = \$350{,}000 \div \$890{,}000 = .393 = 39 \text{ percent}$$

Complete the computation for this second year as you did the first year as follows:

	Col. 1	Col. 2	Col. 3	Col. 4	Col. 5	Col. 6
	Materials cost at FIFO	Completion factor	Col. 1 × Col. 2	Labor and overhead: purchases ratio	Col. 4 × Col. 3	Col. 1 + Col. 5
Raw materials	70,000	0	0	.39	0	70,000
Work in process	35,000	.75	26,250	.39	10,238	45,238
Finished goods	50,000	1.00	50,000	.39	19,500	69,500
Total	155,000		76,250		29,738	184,738

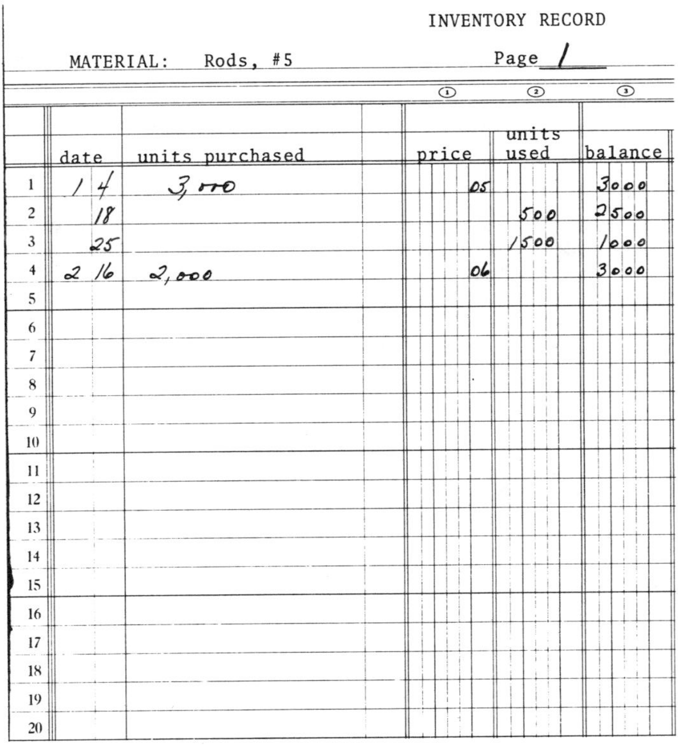

INVENTORY RECORD

MATERIAL: Rods, #5 Page 1

	date	units purchased	price	units used	balance
1	1 4	3,000	05		3000
2	18			500	2500
3	25			1500	1000
4	2 16	2,000	06		3000
5					
6					
7					
8					
9					
10					
11					
12					
13					
14					
15					
16					
17					
18					
19					
20					

FIGURE 13.4. Perpetual inventory record for raw materials.

PERPETUAL INVENTORY RECORDS

You may wish to keep a perpetual inventory of raw materials for reordering purposes. It will also help you compute the value of your year end inventory. The perpetual inventory card shown in Figure 13.4 gives you information at a glance as to when you purchased a particular material, its price, and a current balance of quantity in stock. You should set up an inventory sheet for each kind of raw material, small tools, supplies, etc., which you regularly purchase.

Periodically (at least once a year) you should take a physical inventory of your raw materials to check the accuracy of your perpetual inventory records. Comparing actual physical inventory against perpetual records is a good way to see if you're suffering losses due to theft. You may find, however, that differences between perpetual records and the physical count are due to clerical errors.

SUMMING UP

The most important thing in manufacturing accounting is to ascertain accurately the cost of goods sold. With this knowledge you'll be able to intelligently price your products, and make informed management decisions. This means you must separate manufacturing expenses from sales and administrative expenses. Doing so will inform you as to which costs are incurred in making your products, selling your products, and administering your business.

14

Managerial Accounting

Financial statements can do more than simply tell you your net profit for the year. By studying and comparing various parts of these statements, you can get feedback about your business's past performance and make judgments about its potential performance. This chapter will cover several standard measures of liquidity and profitability. You'll see how to compare financial statements with those of prior years and with those of other businesses in your field. Noticing trends and changes can help you pinpoint a problem area or recognize outstanding achievement early. The last section of this chapter covers break-even analysis—a good tool for analyzing the effect on profits of different costs, operating conditions, methods of pricing, and other management policies.

SEPARATING CURRENT ASSETS AND LIABILITIES FROM LONG-TERM ASSETS AND LIABILITIES

In order for you to use the management tools in this chapter, your assets and liabilities on your Balance Sheet must be broken down as follows:

Current assets. Cash and other assets such as inventories and accounts receivables which will be consumed or converted to cash within one year. Prepaid supplies and expenses are also considered current assets.

Long-term investments. Stocks, bonds, and promissory notes that will be held for more than one year.

Fixed assets. Equipment, buildings, land, and property improvements.

Current liabilities. Debts and other obligations that must be paid within one year.

Long-term liabilities. Debts that are not payable until after one year from the Balance Sheet date.

Figure 14.1 shows a Balance Sheet with these assets and liabilities listed separately.

ABC COMPANY

BALANCE SHEET AS OF 12/31/97

Current Assets		
Cash		$20,000
Accounts Receivable		12,000
Prepaid Expenses		300
Deposits		150
Inventory		20,000
Total Current Assets		52,450
Long-Term Investments		
Notes Receivable		2,000
Fixed Assets		
Equipment	25,000	
Vehicles	10,000	
Equipment & Vehicles	35,000	
Less Accumulated Depreciation	8,000	
Total Fixed Assets		27,000
Total Assets		$81,450

Current Liabilities		
Loans Payable		$ 3,000
Accounts Payable		17,000
Sales Taxes Payable		250
Salary & Payroll Taxes Payable		400
Deferred Revenues		1,000
Total Current Liabilities		21,650
Long-Term Liabilities		
Loans Payable		22,000
Total Liabilities		43,650
Owner's Equity		
Owner's Capital	22,000	
Retained Earnings	15,800	
Total Owner's Equity		37,800
Liabilities + Owner's Equity		$81,450

FIGURE 14.1. Balance Sheet in which assets have been broken down into current assets, long-term investments, and fixed assets. Liabilities have been broken down into current and long-term liabilities.

MEASURES OF LIQUIDITY

Liquidity means simply the ability to pay your bills. If, for example, all your cash is tied up in assets which cannot be converted to cash easily or you have incurred heavy liabilities, or both, you may have difficulty paying your bills as they become due, and therefore have poor liquidity.

Working Capital. Working capital is a company's current assets less its current liabilities. Adequate working capital allows a company to carry sufficient inventories, meet current debts, and take advantage of cash discounts. A lack of sufficient working capital has been the downfall of many businesses.

How much working capital you should have, of course, depends on the nature of your business. Cash planning and budgeting (see Chapter 15) will help in this decision making.

ABC Company's working capital (Figure 14.1) is

$$\text{current assets} - \text{current liabilities} = 52{,}450 - 21{,}650 = 30{,}800$$

To get a further perspective on the adequacy of ABC Company's working capital, let's look at the current ratio.

Current Ratio. The current ratio tells you whether your business has enough current assets to meet its current debts, with a margin of safety for possible losses such as inventory shrinkage or uncollectible accounts receivable.

$$\text{current ratio} = \frac{\text{current assets}}{\text{current liabilities}}$$

Using the Balance Sheet items from Figure 14.1, ABC Company's current ratio is

$$\frac{52{,}450}{21{,}650} = 2.42 \qquad \text{(or 2.42:1)}$$

Is this a good current ratio? The rule of thumb is that the current ratio should be at least two to one. If you decide that your current ratio is too low, you may be able to raise it by

1. Increasing your current assets by taking out a loan with a maturity of *more than one year.*

2. Converting noncurrent assets into current assets (for example, selling some of your fixed assets, or taking out a mortgage on them).
3. Plowing back profits (putting more of your profits back into the business rather than taking them out).
4. Investing more capital in your business (your own or other people's).

Acid Test or Quick Ratio. The quick ratio compares "quick assets" of cash, accounts receivable, short-term notes receivable, and marketable securities to current liabilities. Let us look at ABC Company's quick ratio:

Quick assets:	20,000 cash
	+ 12,000 accounts receivable
	32,000 quick assets

$$\text{Quick ratio} = \frac{\text{quick assets}}{\text{current liabilities}} = \frac{32{,}000}{21{,}650} = 1.48 \qquad \text{(or 1.48:1)}$$

The rule of thumb for quick ratios is that they should be at least one to one. The ABC Company's quick ratio is about one and one-half to one, which is better.

The above measures of liquidity are guidelines only. For example, if you can't collect your accounts receivable, or your inventory is made up of obsolete stock, the current and quick ratios will not mean much. Accounts receivable and inventory turnover rates will add further information to your analysis.

Accounts Receivable Turnover. Accounts receivable turnover tells you the number of times per year you collect your average accounts receivable. From this information, you can compute your average collection period, or number of days' sales tied up in accounts receivable. You will need information from your Income Statement (see Figure 14.2) as well as your Balance Sheet for this.

METHOD 1

$$\frac{\text{yearly sales}}{\text{accounts receivable}} = \frac{100{,}000}{12{,}000}$$

$$= 8.3 \text{ accounts receivable turnover}$$

$$\text{average collection period} = \frac{365 \text{ days}}{8.3} = 44 \text{ days}$$

METHOD 2

$$\text{average sales per day} = \frac{\text{sales}}{\text{days in accounting period}}$$

$$= \frac{100{,}000}{365} = 274 \text{ average sales per day}$$

$$\text{average collection period} = \frac{\text{accounts receivable}}{\text{average sales per day}}$$

$$= \frac{12{,}000}{274} = 44 \text{ days}$$

ABC COMPANY
INCOME STATEMENT 1/1/97 TO 12/31/97

Sales		$100,000
Cost of Goods Sold		
Beginning Inventory	18,000	
plus Purchases	60,000	
less Ending Inventory	20,000	
Cost of Goods Sold		58,000
Gross Margin		42,000
Operating Expenses		
Payroll Expense	18,000	
Rent	3,600	
Utilities	600	
Advertising	2,400	
Supplies	400	
Sales Taxes	500	
Depreciation Expense	1,300	
Miscellaneous Expense	200	
Operating Expenses		27,000
Net Earnings		15,000
Less Owner's Withdrawal		12,000
Earnings After Owner's Withdrawal		$ 3,000
Retained Earnings, Beginning of Year		12,800
Retained Earnings, End of Year		$ 15,800

FIGURE 14.2. Income Statement used for the analyses in this chapter.

In other words, it takes the ABC Company an average of 44 days to collect an account. Is this good or bad? It depends on what terms ABC Company offers its customers. If its terms are 60 days, having a 44-day average collection period is very good. If its terms are 30 days, it is not so good. The rule of thumb is that the average collection period should not exceed 1⅓ times the credit terms. If the ABC Company offers 30 days to pay, its average collection period should be no more than 40 days (30 × 1⅓).

To get a more accurate accounts receivable turnover rate, you can proceed as follows:

1. Use only credit (not cash) sales for the sales figure.
2. Use an *average* accounts receivable figure.

$$\frac{\text{accounts receivable at beginning of year} + \text{accounts receivable at end of year}}{2}$$

(See Chapter 7, "Credit and Collections," for a further discussion of the importance of and methods of keeping control over accounts receivable)

Inventory Turnover. Inventory turnover shows how fast your merchandise is moving. It is found by dividing the cost of goods sold by average inventory:

$$\text{ABC Company average inventory} = \frac{\text{beginning inventory} + \text{ending inventory}}{2}$$

$$= \frac{18{,}000 + 20{,}000}{2} = 19{,}000$$

$$\text{inventory turnover} = \frac{\text{cost of goods sold}}{\text{average inventory}}$$

$$= \frac{58{,}000}{19{,}000} = 3$$

Thus the ABC Company "turned" its inventories three times during the year, or used up merchandise totaling three times its average inventory investment. Usually, the higher the turnover, the better. It is considered a mark of good merchandising and means that a smaller investment in inventory is required. It means items are moving quickly off the shelves. However, at the other extreme a high inventory turnover can mean that you aren't keeping adequate stock on hand and will lose customers. You should compare your inventory turnover with that of other companies similar to yours.

(Note: When using the above tools for measuring liquidity, keep in mind that ratios are not ends in themselves and must be interpreted with care. Since ratios are based on past performance, use them in the light of your best knowledge and judgment about the future. Compare your company's ratios with those of similar businesses. Ask your local or national trade association for published data from members. Also see published ratios and turnover figures such as those put out by Dun and Bradstreet. Be aware, however, that there are different ways of computing and recording some of the items on financial statements, which means the figures for your business may not correspond exactly to those of another.)

MEASURES OF PROFITABILITY

Is your business earning as much profit as it should, considering the amount of money invested in it? A number of ratios have been devised to help you measure your company's success in achieving this financial objective.

Asset Earning Power. The ratio of net profit (earnings) to total assets is a guide for appraising the overall earning power of your company's assets. For ABC Company,

$$\text{asset earning power} = \frac{\text{net profits}}{\text{total assets}} = \frac{15{,}000}{81{,}450} = .184 \qquad \text{or 18.4 percent}$$

Return on Owner's Equity. This ratio shows the return you received on your own investment in the business. In computing this ratio, you would use an average owner's equity figure. For ABC Company,

$$\text{average owner's equity} = \frac{\text{owner's equity beginning of year} + \text{owner's equity end of year}}{2}$$

$$= \frac{34{,}800 + 37{,}800}{2} = 36{,}300$$

$$\text{return on equity} = \frac{\text{net profit}}{\text{average owner's equity}}$$

$$= \frac{15{,}000}{36{,}300} = .41 \qquad \text{or 41 percent}$$

It is important to realize that the return on owner's equity for a proprietorship and partnership will usually be higher than for a corporation, because an owner-manager's salary is an allowable expense for a corporation. The owner's equity of a corporation will consist of capital stock and retained earnings. The net profit if ABC Company were incorporated would show the $12,000 owner's withdrawal as part of Payroll Expense and the net profit would be only $3,000. Using this profit figure, the return on equity would be

$$\frac{3{,}000}{36{,}300} = .083 \qquad \text{or 8.3 percent}$$

In other words, as owner-manager of the ABC Company in either case, you're earning $12,000 for managing the company and 8.3 percent per year return on the $36,300 capital invested in the business. Could you earn more than 8.3 percent by investing this money somewhere else? You may be willing to settle for a low return on equity in order to be doing what you want—running your own business—but you should at least be aware of what your money is earning for you.

Net Profit on Sales. This ratio measures the difference between what your company takes in and what it spends in the process of doing business. The ratio depends mainly on two factors: operating costs and pricing policies. If your net profits on sales go down, for instance, it might be because you have lowered prices in the hope of increasing your total sales volume. Or it might be that your costs have been creeping up while prices remained the same. For the ABC Company,

$$\text{net profit on sales} = \frac{\text{net profit}}{\text{net sales}} = \frac{15{,}000}{100{,}000} = .15 \qquad \text{or 15 percent}$$

This means that for every dollar of sales, the company has made a profit of 15 cents.

This ratio is most useful when you compare your figures with those of businesses similar to yours, or when you study the trends in your own business from year to year or month to month. Comparing the net profit on sales for individual products or product lines is also useful. Such an analysis will help you decide which products or lines should be pushed.

Remember, when comparing your net profit on sales with other companies, again it makes a big difference whether you are a corporation, a proprietorship, or a partnership. Owner's salary is part of net profits in proprietorships and partnerships, but not in corporations. Most published ratios are for corporations.

COMPARATIVE FINANCIAL STATEMENTS

In order to see changes from month to month or year to year, it's useful to prepare comparative financial statements showing two or more accounting periods side by side, with the amount and percentage of increase or decrease. Figures 14.3 and 14.4 illustrate a comparative Balance Sheet and Income Statement for the ABC Company. To compute the increase or decrease, you subtract the earlier year from the later year figure. To compute the percentage change, you divide this difference by the earlier year figure.

You should examine changes in financial statements from period to period in order to determine the reason for them and whether they are favorable or unfavorable. It may be favorable, for example, if Sales go up, but not if Gross Profit goes down at the same time. In general, you'll find comparative Income Statements more useful than comparative Balance Sheets.

COMMON-SIZE COMPARATIVE STATEMENTS

On a common-size Income Statement, net sales are assigned a 100-percent value and then each item is shown as a percentage of net sales. Comparing Income Statements in common-size form can be a useful analytical tool. Having items broken down by percentages of Sales helps pinpoint their relative change.

For example, in Figure 14.5 you'll see that cost of goods sold changed from 58 percent of sales in 1997 to 57.5 percent in 1998; advertising changed from 2.4 percent of sales in 1997 to 2.8 percent in 1998; and so on.

BREAK-EVEN ANALYSIS

The "break-even point" is the point of sales volume at which sales revenues just cover costs, with no profit and no loss. Break-even analysis can show at what approximate level of sales a new product will pay for itself and begin to bring in a profit. It's also helpful in analyzing the profitability of products already being sold. Suppose you have a product that has passed its peak in popularity. It's still fairly profitable, but the demand for it is slacking off. Break-even analysis can show you about how far sales can drop before the item will stop making any profit at all, and below what level it will no longer cover even its fixed costs.

Break-even analysis helps to answer questions such as

1. How many units of the new product will have to be sold, given estimates of its cost and selling price, if we are to break even?

ABC COMPANY

COMPARATIVE BALANCE SHEET FOR 1997 AND 1998

	1997	1998	Increase or Decrease	Percentage Change
Current Assets				
Cash	$20,000	$16,000	$(4,000)	(20%)
Accounts Receivable	12,000	15,000	3,000	25
Prepaid Expenses	300	400	100	33⅓
Deposits	150	150	0	0
Inventory	20,000	26,000	6,000	30
Total Current Assets	52,450	57,550	5,100	9.7
Long-Term Investments				
Notes Receivable	2,000	1,400	(600)	(30)
Fixed Assets				
Equipment	25,000	34,000	9,000	36
Vehicles	10,000	10,000	0	0
Less Depreciation	8,000	10,000	2,000	25
Total Fixed Assets	27,000	34,000	7,000	26
Total Assets	$81,450	$92,950	$11,500	14
Current Liabilities				
Loans Payable	$ 3,000	$ 600	$(2,400)	(80)
Accounts Payable	17,000	18,000	1,000	6
Sales Taxes Payable	250	300	50	20
Salaries & Payroll Taxes Payable	400	500	100	25
Deferred Revenues	1,000	1,500	500	50
Total Current Liabilities	21,650	20,900	(750)	(3.5)
Long-Term Liabilities				
Loans Payable	22,000	31,150	9,150	41.6
Total Liabilities	43,650	52,050	8,400	19
Owner's Equity				
Owner's Capital	22,000	22,000	0	0
Retained Earnings	15,800	18,900	3,100	20
Total Owner's Capital & Retained Earnings	37,800	40,900	3,100	8
Owner's Equity + Liabilities	$81,450	$92,950	$11,500	14

FIGURE 14.3. Comparison of 1997 and 1998 Balance Sheet figures for the ABC Company.

ABC COMPANY

COMPARATIVE INCOME STATEMENT FOR 1997 AND 1998

	1997	1998	Increase or Decrease	Percentage Change
Sales	$100,000	$120,000	$20,000	20%
Cost of Goods Sold				
Beginning Inventory	18,000	20,000	2,000	11
plus Purchases	60,000	75,000	15,000	25
less Ending Inventory	20,000	26,000	6,000	30
Cost of Goods Sold	58,000	69,000	11,000	19
Gross Margin	42,000	51,000	9,000	21.4
Operating Expenses				
Payroll	18,000	21,000	3,000	16.7
Rent	3,600	3,600	0	0
Utilities	600	700	100	16.7
Advertising	2,400	3,300	900	37.5
Supplies	400	500	100	25
Sales Taxes	500	700	200	40
Depreciation Expense	1,300	2,000	700	53.8
Miscellaneous Expense	200	300	100	50
Operating Expenses	27,000	32,100	5,100	18.9
Net Earnings	$ 15,000	$ 18,900	$ 3,900	26

FIGURE 14.4. Comparison of 1997 and 1998 Income Statement figures for the ABC Company.

2. The change we are planning will mean a 10-percent increase in fixed costs. What effect will this have on profits?
3. What will be the effect of a 5-percent reduction in selling price (or a 15-percent decline in the number of units sold)?
4. How much more will we have to sell to make up for a 15-cent hourly increase in wages?
5. If we buy the new machine we are considering (or truck, or building improvement), how long will it be before the investment pays for itself and begins to return a profit?

ABC COMPANY

COMMON-SIZE COMPARATIVE INCOME STATEMENT FOR 1997 AND 1998

	1997	1998	Percent of Sales 1997	Percent of Sales 1998
Sales	$100,000	$120,000	100%	100%
Cost of Goods Sold				
Beginning Inventory	18,000	20,000	18.0	16.7
plus Purchases	60,000	75,000	60.0	62.5
less Ending Inventory	20,000	26,000	20.0	21.7
Cost of Goods Sold	58,000	69,000	58.0	57.5
Gross Margin	42,000	51,000	42.0	42.5
Operating Expenses				
Payroll	18,000	21,000	18.0	17.5
Rent	3,600	3,600	3.6	3.0
Utilities	600	700	0.6	0.6
Advertising	2,400	3,300	2.4	2.8
Supplies	400	500	0.4	0.4
Sales Taxes	500	700	0.5	0.6
Depreciation Expense	1,300	2,000	1.3	1.7
Miscellaneous Expense	200	300	0.2	0.3
Operating Expenses	27,000	32,100	27.0	26.8
Net Earnings	$ 15,000	$ 18,900	15.0	15.8

FIGURE 14.5. Comparison of common-size Income Statement figures for 1997 and 1998 for the ABC Company.

Three Types of Costs. Costs can be classified as fixed, variable, or semivariable. Fixed costs do not vary with the level of business activity. Examples of fixed costs are sales and administrative (not plant) salaries, property insurance, property taxes, depreciation expense, management salaries, and so on. No matter how much business you do, they stay the same. Variable costs vary directly with the volume of business activity. They double when production is doubled, or drop to zero if there is no production. Plant (manufacturing) labor and materials are examples of variable costs for a manufacturer. Cost of goods sold is a variable cost for a retailer or wholesaler; the more you sell, the more inventory you use up, thereby directly increasing your cost of goods sold. For example, if cost of goods sold is \$60.00 for \$100.00 worth of sales, it will probably take \$120.00 cost of goods sold for \$200 worth of sales:

$$2 \times 100 = 200 \qquad 2 \times 60 = 120$$

Semivariable costs change with the level of business activity, but not in direct proportion. Office equipment might be an example, or salespeople's salaries. Up to a point these costs are about the same regardless of sales. Beyond that point, they go up. For example, a salesperson might be able to handle an increase in sales up to a certain point, but beyond that there may be too many customers for one person to handle efficiently. A full- or part-time assistant may have to be hired.

You'll have to break down semivariable costs into their fixed and variable components in order to use the break-even formula.

Finding The Break-Even Point. Once you've identified and classified all costs as fixed or variable, you can find the break-even point by using the following formula:

$$\text{break-even volume} = \frac{\text{total fixed costs}}{\text{selling price} - \text{variable costs per unit}}$$

Suppose the RJK Manufacturing Company has figured the costs on one of its products as follows:

Total fixed costs: \$40,000
Variable costs: \$20 per unit

The selling price is \$40 per unit.

$$\text{break-even volume} = \frac{40{,}000}{40 - 20} = 2{,}000 \text{ units}$$

This means that 2,000 units will have to be sold just to break even:

Costs on 2,000 units:	40,000 fixed costs
	+ 40,000 variable costs (2,000 × 20)
	80,000 total costs
Sales revenue:	80,000 (2,000 units × 40 sales price per unit)
	− 80,000 total costs
	0 profit

The more units the RJK Manufacturing Company sells beyond 2,000, the greater percentage of profit they will make on the items (provided fixed costs remain the same). For example, (a) If 3,000 units are sold,

Sales revenue:	120,000 (3,000 × 40)
Total costs:	100,000 (40,000 + 3,000 × 20)
Profit:	20,000

(b) If 6,000 units are sold,

Sales revenue:	240,000 (6,000 × 40)
Total costs:	160,000 (40,000 + 6,000 × 20)
Profit:	80,000

Note that sales doubled from 3,000 to 6,000 units, whereas profit quadrupled from \$20,000 to \$80,000. This is because the only cost for the 3,000 additional units was the variable cost of \$60,000 (3,000 × \$20) and the additional revenue was \$120,000 (3,000 × \$40).

At some point as sales increase, fixed costs will probably change. For example, you can only display so much merchandise in a certain amount of square feet of selling space. Or when a machine is being utilized 24 hours a day, you cannot increase production without buying another machine.

Another way to use break-even analysis is when you want to know what your minimum sales will have to be in order to break even. Suppose, for example, you are in the mail-order business. You want to place an ad for gidgets. The ad will cost \$500. You want to know how many orders (sales) you will need for this ad in order to break even (cover all your costs). You pay \$2.00 for each gidget, plus 25 cents each for mailing and handling. Your sales price is \$5.00 each. How many orders must you get to break even?

Fixed costs:	500 ad
Variable costs per unit:	2.00 cost of gidget
	+ .25 mailing and handling
	2.25 total variable costs

$$\text{break-even volume} = \frac{\text{total fixed costs}}{\text{selling price} - \text{variable costs per unit}}$$

$$= \frac{500}{5.00 - 2.25} = 182 \text{ units}$$

In other words, 182 orders generated by this ad will cover the cost of the ad plus all costs of supplying the 182 gidgets.

By being aware of fixed and variable costs and their relationship to increases and decreases in sales or production volume, you'll be able to plan better for future expansion of your business.

SUMMING UP

Managerial accounting consists of taking the financial information you have compiled for your business and analyzing it. Measures of liquidity, measures of profitability, comparative financial statements, and break-even analysis are all tools you can use to help you make decisions about the future direction your business should take.

15

Cash Budgeting And Financial Planning

Preparing a cash budget is simply listing how much cash you expect to come in, to go out, and to have left over (or need). By seeing ahead of time that you will have extra cash, you can plan for short-term investments. If you see that you will be short in the future, you can start to plan for short-term loans. If you see that you will be short of cash over a long period, you may need a long-term loan or further capital investment; another solution to a cash shortage is to cut back on expansions such as the purchase of a new asset or opening of a new store.

Although the cash budget will show you where your money is going and how much is needed each month (year), financial planning includes the preparation of a projected income statement and balance sheet. The income statement is especially important. Listing expected sales and expenses helps you decide how much cash you will need. It also gives you something by which to measure actual performance. A projected balance sheet puts in black and white exactly where you expect your company to stand in terms of assets and liabilities in one year.

Taken together, the cash budget and projected financial statements give you an overall picture of your company's future, in terms of cash flow, investment potential, borrowing needs, asset acquisitions, marketing goals, and operating expense limits. By applying the managerial accounting tools discussed in Chapter 14 to your financial planning, in addition to your own experience and judgment, you'll be in a better position to foresee problems and take advantage of opportunities in your company's future.

CASH BUDGET

You should set up a cash budget form as illustrated in Figure 15.1. The example is for a three-month cash budget, but you can set one up for the entire year if you wish. First, list all the items that bring in cash, then the expected

CASH BUDGET

For three months ending March 31, 19 ______

		JANUARY		FEBRUARY		MARCH	
		Budget	Actual	Budget	Actual	Budget	Actual
1	Beg. Balance						
2							
3	Cash Receipts:						
4	Cash Sales						
5	A.R. Collect.						
6	Other Income						
7	Total Cash Rec.						
8							
9	Cash Payments:						
10	Purchases						
11	Payroll						
12	Rent						
13	Utilities						
14	Advertising						
15	Loan Paymts.						
16	Sales Taxes						
17	Asset Purch.						
18	Supplies						
19	Misc.						
20	Total Cash Pmts:						
21							
22	Ending. Bal.						
23							

FIGURE 15.1. Three-month Cash Budget Form. You may wish to prepare one for six or twelve months at a time.

outlays of cash, and, finally, the balance. If your cash balance is negative, or too low to allow a safe margin, you should consider a short-term loan. If you have extra cash, you can consider a short-term investment.

The balance at the end of one month becomes the beginning balance of the following month. Note that there's a column in which to list your *actual* cash receipts and payments as they occur. These actual figures can be used to make any necessary modifications in the following months' budgets. If you find your budget out of line with what actually is happening, it's time to find out what's going wrong. Are sales much lower or greater than you expected? Are you having difficulty collecting accounts receivable? Have any of your expenses risen drastically?

As mentioned in Chapter 14, having enough working capital to pay your bills is crucial to the success of your business. If you're constantly scraping the barrel for cash to meet a payroll or pay a creditor—getting by by the skin of your teeth—you are putting your whole business in jeopardy. A banker will think more favorably of your loan request if you make it three months *before* a crisis arises rather than the day *after* it happens.

Although we generally expect most problems to arise in the area of not having *enough* cash, sometimes the opposite happens. Leaving large sums of unnecessary capital in your business checking account is a waste. If the measures of liquidity in Chapter 14 tell you that you have much more working capital than necessary, especially in cash form, you should consider putting this capital to work in some short-term investments. By being *too* conservative, you may miss an opportunity to have your investment work to capacity for you.

PROJECTED INCOME STATEMENT

Figure 15.2 illustrates a projected Income Statement for a service business. Figure 15.3 shows one for a retail operation (the same format applies to wholesale businesses). The easiest way to prepare projected Income Statements is to base your plans on what happened in the past. If sales have increased 10 percent a year over the last four years, you can use this information to prepare your projected sales figure. Then you can use the percentages of sales from your common-size Income Statement (see Chapter 14) to compute cost of goods sold, and other variable costs. For example, if 1997 sales are $100,000 and you expect a 10-percent increase in 1998,

10 percent of $100,000 = $10,000
$100,000 + $10,000 = $110,000 sales projected for 1998

DEF SERVICE COMPANY
PROJECTED INCOME STATEMENT
FOR 1/1/98 TO 12/31/98

Revenues		$40,000
Operating Expenses		
Salaries	12,000	
Supplies	2,200	
Rent	3,000	
Utilities	600	
Advertising	2,500	
Depreciation Expense	900	
Interest Expense	300	
Insurance Expense	400	
Miscellaneous Expense	800	
Total Operating Expenses		22,700
Net Earnings		$17,300

FIGURE 15.2. Projected Income Statement for a service business.

If advertising expenses have always been four percent of sales in the past,

four percent of $110,000 = .04 × $110,000
= $4,400 projected advertising expense for 1998

The past cannot always be used to predict the future, however. Sales increases do not just "happen" by themselves. During an economic downturn, sales may decline. With the introduction of a better marketing plan, sales may shoot ahead of past performance. So you need to use your judgment about the economy, competition, increases in sales force, new product lines, etc., when choosing a sales figure for your projected Income Statement.

After that, you can use the percentages in your common-size Income Statement as a guideline for the rest of the figures. Here, too, if you know that merchandise prices are going up faster than the sales prices, you may have to allot a greater percentage for cost of goods sold. In another instance you may have purchased a machine that will eliminate some of your labor costs, making this figure lower, but depreciation expenses higher. So use your common-size Income Statement as a guide, but add input from your own knowledge and management plans for the future. Fixed costs such as

IJK RETAIL STORE
PROJECTED INCOME STATEMENT
FOR 1/1/98 TO 12/31/98

Gross Sales	$83,200	
Less Sales Taxes	(3,200)	
Net Sales		$80,000
Cost of Goods Sold		
Beginning Inventory	15,000	
plus Purchases	51,000	
less Ending Inventory	(16,000)	
Cost of Goods Sold		50,000
Gross Profit Margin		30,000
Operating Expenses		
Salaries	7,000	
Rent	3,600	
Utilities	400	
Advertising	2,400	
Depreciation Expense	600	
Interest Expense	100	
Supplies Expense	200	
Insurance Expense	400	
Total Operating Expenses		14,700
Net Earnings		$15,300

FIGURE 15.3. Projected Income Statement for a retail store.

rent and depreciation should be estimated based on expected rental increases or the amount of equipment you expect to buy.

PROJECTED BALANCE SHEET

Figure 15.4 shows a projected Balance Sheet for the DEF Service Company. Figure 15.5 shows one for the IJK Retail Store. To prepare a projected Balance Sheet, begin with the last actual Balance Sheet you prepared. Some items may remain the same, while others will change.

Fixed assets will remain the same except for accumulated depreciation, which will be higher (add the depreciation expense from your projected Income Statement). If you plan to buy additional fixed assets, total fixed assets

DEF SERVICE COMPANY
PROJECTED BALANCE SHEET AS OF 12/31/98

Current Assets			*Current Liabilities*		
Cash		$ 6,000	Salaries Payable		$ 150
Deposits		100	Notes Payable		250
Prepaid Supplies		200	Total Current Liabilities		400
Total Current Assets		6,300			
			Long-Term Liabilities		
Fixed Assets			Loans Payable		20,000
Equipment	40,000				
Vehicle	12,000		*Total Liabilities*		20,400
Equipment & Vehicles	52,000		*Owner's Equity*		
Less Accumulated			Owner's Capital	15,000	
Depreciation	10,000		Retained Earnings	12,900	
Total Fixed Assets		42,000	Total Owner's Equity		27,900
Total Assets		$48,300	*Liabilities + Owner's Equity*		$48,300

FIGURE 15.4. Projected Balance Sheet for a service business.

IJK RETAIL STORE

PROJECTED BALANCE SHEET AS OF 12/31/98

Current Assets		
Cash		$10,000
Inventory		16,000
Prepaid Expenses		300
Total Current Assets		26,300
Fixed Assets		
Store Equipment	48,000	
Vehicle	8,000	
Equipment & Vehicles	56,000	
Less Accumulated Depreciation	12,000	
Total Fixed Assets		44,000
Total Assets		$70,300

Current Liabilities		
Accounts Payable		$ 8,000
Notes Payable		600
Salaries Payable		200
Sales Taxes Payable		500
Total Current Liabilities		9,300
Long-Term Liabilities		
Loans Payable		26,000
Total Liabilities		35,300
Owner's Equity		
Owner's Capital	20,000	
Retained Earnings	15,000	
Total Owner's Equity		35,000
Liabilities + Owner's Equity		$70,300

FIGURE 15.5. Projected Balance Sheet for a retail store.

will increase by the purchase price of the asset. For example, if you purchase a $10,000 machine and fixed assets were $40,000 at the end of the year, they will be $50,000 on the projected Balance Sheet for the following year (be sure to add the extra depreciation expense for this $10,000 machine to accumulated depreciation).

Accounts receivable will probably increase proportionately as credit sales increase, unless there is some other reason for them to change, such as more effective collection procedures or a lengthening or shortening of credit terms.

Cash can be taken from the final balance for the end of the year on your cash budget (see above). The cash figure on your Balance Sheet will be influenced by expenditures, new loans and notes, owner's withdrawals, etc.

Items such as deposits, prepaid supplies, and prepaid expenses will probably be the same or similar, and accuracy here is not that important since these items usually make up a small percentage of total assets.

Any changes in notes or loans receivable will depend on payments made to you by debtors, and new loans or notes (again, see your cash budget).

For an inventory figure, you can use the same figure as your ending inventory the prior year unless you expect changes in the amount of inventory you'll keep in stock the following year. For example, if you plan to carry an average addition of 10 percent more inventory in stock, and last year's ending inventory was $20,000, a projected ending inventory figure for the next year would be $22,000 (10 percent × $20,000 = $2,000; $20,000 + $2,000 = $22,000). If sales volume increases, either your average inventory or turnover rate, or both, have to increase. Be sure your projected Balance Sheet inventory figure matches the ending inventory figure on your projected Income Statement.

Under liabilities, loans payable will be decreased by whatever payments are made during the year and increased by the amount of any new loans taken out. You must be sure to list loan payments on your cash budget. Accounts payable will probably increase proportionately as ending inventory does. Accrued liabilities for payroll, taxes, etc., will probably be about the same as the year before.

Under owner's equity, owner's capital always remains the same, unless new capital investments are made. Retained earnings will be increased by the net earnings on your projected Income Statement less owner's withdrawal.

When making your projected Balance Sheet, play around with the figures in pencil first so you can make changes. Use information from your cash budget, projected Income Statement, and prior Balance Sheet to help you arrive at projected Balance Sheet figures. Remember that total assets must match total liabilities plus owner's equity. If you add something to one side of the equation, you must add it to the other (or subtract it from another item on the same side of the equation).

SUMMING UP

Preparing a cash budget on a monthly basis is vital to the stability of a company's operation. It allows you to plan for greater cash needs during busy seasons or periods of expansion by applying for loans ahead of time. It also shows you when you will have extra cash available for short-term investments.

Projected financial statements put in writing the objectives and expectations you have for your business's future. Managerial accounting, cash budgeting, and projected financial statements are a combination approach giving you control and direction over your company's life and growth.

16
Partnership Accounting

If your company is a partnership, separate Capital and Withdrawal accounts must be kept for each partner. If no other agreement has been made, the law provides that all partnership earnings and losses are to be shared equally; but the partners may agree in advance to any method of sharing earnings and losses. If they make an agreement as to how earnings are to be shared, but say nothing of losses, losses are shared in the same way as earnings.

At the end of every year, your company's profits (or losses) must be distributed to each partner's Capital account. Partners, like sole proprietors, cannot actually receive a "salary" from their company. A partner works for partnership profits. You may, however, wish to allocate "salaries" or "interest" payments, or both, to partners as a way of compensating each one fairly for time and capital invested in the business. Two methods of distributing profits are discussed below, but the same principles can be applied to any method you choose.

FRACTIONAL BASIS OF ALLOCATING EARNINGS

The easiest way to divide partnership earnings is to assign each partner a fraction, equal or otherwise. For example, two partners could take one half each, one quarter and three quarters, two thirds and one third, etc. You may wish to make an unequal distribution if one partner contributes a greater share of the starting capital, or contributes more time to the business's operation.

For example, let's assume Smith and Jones have a partnership in which Smith contributed $20,000 and Jones $10,000 starting capital. Smith is managing the business full time and Jones works for it three quarters of the time. They decide to divide earnings two thirds to Smith, and one third to Jones.

When the $30,000 is invested, the Owner's Capital accounts will show the following:

SMITH CAPITAL

debit (−)	credit (+)
	20,000

JONES CAPITAL

debit (−)	credit (+)
	10,000

(Note: Cash will have been debited with the $30,000.)

At the end of the year, Smith and Jones Company has earned $9,000 profit. It will be distributed as follows:

$$\tfrac{2}{3} \times \$9{,}000 = \$6{,}000 \text{ to Smith}$$
$$\tfrac{1}{3} \times \$9{,}000 = \$3{,}000 \text{ to Jones}$$

If no withdrawals were made during the year, the total $9,000 would be credited to Smith and Jones Capital accounts as follows:

SMITH CAPITAL

debit (−)	credit (+)
	20,000 *
	6,000

JONES CAPITAL

debit (−)	credit (+)
	10,000 *
	3,000

* Prior entry.

If the partners have withdrawn money from the partnership, these withdrawals would be debited to their capital accounts, thus reducing their capital. If Smith withdrew $4,000 during the year and Jones withdrew $2,000, their capital accounts would then be $22,000 (Smith) and $11,000 (Jones):

SMITH CAPITAL

debit (−)	credit (+)
4,000	20,000*
	6,000*

JONES CAPITAL

debit (−)	credit (+)
2,000	10,000*
	3,000*

*Prior entry.

If the company suffers a loss, the loss would be divided in the same manner as earnings and debited to each partner's Capital account:

Net loss: $3,000

Smith's share:	⅔ × $3,000 = $2,000
Jones' share:	⅓ × $3,000 = 1,000
	$3,000 total net loss

SMITH CAPITAL

debit (−)	credit (+)
2,000 †	20,000 *

JONES CAPITAL

debit (−)	credit (+)
1,000 †	10,000 *

* Prior entry of capital investment.
† Partner's share of net loss.

BASE SALARIES PLUS EQUAL SHARE ON BALANCE OF PROFIT

You may wish to allow each partner a set "salary" and then divide the remainder of the profits equally. For example, suppose White, Black, and Green have a partnership in which they agree to give White a salary of $10,000, Black $12,000, and Green $14,000, and to split the balance of profits equally. The division of $39,000 net profits would be as follows:

Net profits: $39,000

Green's salary:	$14,000
Black's salary:	$12,000
White's salary:	$10,000
	$36,000 total salaries, leaving a balance of $3,000 from $39,000 profits

⅓ of $3,000 = $1,000 share each of balance of profits

Green's share:	$14,000 + $1,000 = $15,000
Black's share:	$12,000 + $1,000 = $13,000
White's share:	$10,000 + $1,000 = $11,000
	$39,000 total profits

The $15,000, $13,000, and $11,000 would be credited to each partner's Capital account.

If only \$30,000 net profits had been made, the difference between the \$36,000 required for partners' salaries and the net profit would be shared equally:

$$\$36{,}000 - \$30{,}000 = \$6{,}000$$

$$\frac{\$6{,}000}{3} = \$2{,}000 \text{ deducted from each partner's earnings}$$

Green's share:	\$14,000 – \$2,000 = \$12,000
Black's share:	\$12,000 – \$2,000 = \$10,000
White's share:	\$10,000 – \$2,000 = \$ 8,000
	\$30,000 total net profits

FINANCIAL STATEMENTS

A partnership Income Statement would look the same as a propietor's (see Chapter 11) except that the distribution of profits or losses between partners would be listed at the bottom of the statement. Figure 16.1 gives an example of a partnership Income Statement. On the Balance Sheet, partners' Capital accounts are listed separately under partners' equity, as illustrated in Figure 16.2.

LOANS MADE BY PARTNERS TO A PARTNERSHIP

If a partner makes a loan to the partnership, the interest paid on this loan is a deductible business expense for the company, but must be included by the partner as part of his or her income. Even if the partner does not actually take the earned interest out of the company, it must be treated as an accrued expense by the partnership and declared as earnings by the partner.

For example, suppose Green loans his company \$5,000 on a short-term note at 15 percent interest. In six months the company pays him the \$5,000 plus \$375 interest (\$5,000 × 15 percent × one half year). The loan and repayment would be recorded as follows:

(a) loan of \$5,000 made by Green.
(b) \$5,375 loan plus interest paid to Green.

CASH		LOANS PAYABLE		INTEREST EXPENSE	
debit (+)	credit (−)	debit (−)	credit (+)	debit (+)	credit (−)
5,000 (a)	5,375 (b)	5,000 (b)	5,000 (a)	375 (b)	

INCOME STATEMENT 1/1/98 TO 12/31/98

Revenues		$60,000	
Operating Expenses			
Rent	4,800		
Utilities	1,800		
Advertising	3,200		
Insurance	600		
Supplies	3,400		
Depreciation Expense	6,000		
Miscellaneous Expense	1,200		
Total Operating Expenses		21,000	
Net Earnings		$39,000	
Partners' Shares			
Green: Salary	14,000		
+ ⅓ balance profit	1,000		
Total share	15,000		
Less owner's withdrawals	14,000		
	1,000	Balance, Green's share	
Black: Salary	12,000		
+ ⅓ balance profit	1,000		
Total share	13,000		
Less owner's withdrawals	12,000		
	1,000	Balance, Black's share	
White: Salary	10,000		
+ ⅓ balance profit	1,000		
Total share	11,000		
Less owner's withdrawals	10,000		
	1,000	Balance, White's share	

FIGURE 16.1. Partnership Income Statement.

If, by the end of the year, Green had not yet been paid his $375 interest, an adjustment in the company's General Journal would have to be made to account for this accrued expense (see Figure 16.3). It would then appear on the Income Statement as part of Interest Expense and on the Balance Sheet under liabilities as Accrued Interest.

BALANCE SHEET AS OF 12/31/98

Current Assets			*Liabilities*		
Cash		$ 6,000	Loans Payable		$22,500
Prepaid Supplies		400	*Partners' Equity*		
Prepaid Expenses		100	Green's Capital	16,000	
Total Current Assets		6,500	Black's Capital	11,000	
Fixed Assets			White's Capital	11,000	
Building	60,000		Total Partners' Equity		38,000
Less Accumulated Depreciation	6,000				
Total Fixed Assets		54,000			
Total Assets		$60,500	*Liabilities + Parners' Equity*		$60,500

FIGURE 16.2. Balance Sheet for the partners in Figure 16.1

GENERAL JOURNAL Page 1

	date	description	debit	credit
1	12-31	Interest Expense	375 -	
2		Accrued Interest		375 -
3				
4		To account for interest owed		
5		Green on $5,000 - Loan.		
6				
7				
8				
9				
10				
11				
12				
13				
14				
15				
16				
17				
18				
19				
20				

FIGURE 16.3. General Journal entry to make an adjustment for the accrued interest owed a partner on a loan.

INCOME TAXES

Like a proprietorship, a partnership as a business entity is not subject to federal and, in most cases, to state income taxes. The individual partners, however, are taxed on their share of the net earnings of the business. There is a special partnership form (Form 1065), which must be filed by the partnership. Schedules K and K-1 show the partner's share of income, credits, deductions, etc. (See IRS Publication 334, *Tax Guide For Small Business* for complete instructions on filling out these forms and accompanying schedules.)

SUMMING UP

In partnership accounting, each partner's capital investment must be recorded in a separate capital account. At the end of the year, each partner's share of the net profits (or losses) is computed and added to or deducted from his or her Capital account.

The interest paid or accrued on loans made by partners to the business is recorded in an Interest Expense account. This interest is an allowable business expense for the partnership, but must be included as part of the partner's earnings for the year, even if the interest amount has not actually been withdrawn from the business by the partner.

Each partner's share of net earnings is taxed as individual income. There are no federal income taxes to pay as a business entity. Special partnership forms, however, must be filed which show the business's profits (or losses) and how they were distributed to the partners. Just as a proprietor would, partners pay taxes on all earnings of the business whether or not they actually withdraw these funds for personal use.

17

Internal Control

The purpose of internal control procedures is to limit errors, promote efficient operation, and protect your business's assets from waste, fraud, and theft. If you're running a one-person operation in which you do everything yourself—make purchases, receive goods, make payments, etc.—you will be in control. As your business grows, however, and the number of employees increases, it will become more difficult for you to personally oversee all these functions.

This chapter covers several internal control procedures in basic areas such as purchases, receipts, and disbursements. The procedures you use will depend on the type of business you have and on its size. The principles of good internal control are as follows:

1. The clear establishment of each employee's responsibility. For example, if two people have access to the petty cash box and an error is found, it will be difficult to ascertain who is responsible for the error.
2. The maintenance of adequate records and following of the recordkeeping procedures outlined throughout this book in a timely manner.
3. Obtaining adequate casualty insurance on your assets.
4. Dividing duties in the recordkeeping and maintenance of assets in a particular area. For example, you should not have the same employee placing purchase orders, receiving merchandise, and paying vendors.
5. If possible, the rotation of employees in their job functions.
6. The use of mechanical devices such as cash registers, check protectors, and mechanical counters whenever feasible.
7. Employee cooperation, obtained by explaining internal control procedures and why they are necessary.
8. The review of internal control procedures periodically in order to see that they are being followed or, if necessary, that they are changed. (For example, ask yourself, "If I were a dishonest employee, how would I go about stealing from my company?")

CASH RECEIPTS AND SALES

In a retail or service operation, you may wish to use prenumbered sales slips. You can then instruct employees to mark a slip "void" if an error is made and to keep a copy of it. At the end of the day, no numbers should be missing. If you don't follow this procedure, an employee can easily destroy a sales slip and pocket the cash. Using a cash register with a locked-in tape is another way to keep a permanent record of each cash sale.

If you receive checks in the mail from customers, it's wise to separate the processing duties and have different employees:

1. Open the mail.
2. List the checks received.
3. Make bank deposits.
4. Update accounts receivable records.

A type of fraud that can occur if these duties are not separated is called "lapping receivables." A clerk takes the check from A Company and cashes it himself. The next day when B Company's check is received, he credits this payment to A Company's account. The next day when C Company's check is received, he credits this payment to B Company's account, and so forth. This way it takes a long time to uncover his theft.

When shipping goods to customers, you should establish the following procedures:

1. Use prenumbered invoices.
2. Make sure everything shipped was billed to the customer and that everything billed was shipped.
3. Do not have the same person prepare invoices, ship merchandise, and bill the customer.
4. Require backup material such as bills of lading, UPS receipts, etc., to verify shipment before customers are billed.

If you have an outside sales force or use commissioned sales representatives, do not allow them to collect checks, but rather have customers send checks to you directly and be sure your company address in on invoices. When a sales representative sends you a customer's order, send out a confirming order directly to the customer before shipping any merchandise. This single procedure would have saved one company $6,000 in losses from a crooked sales representative who sent in phony orders from nonexistent customers and had merchandise delivered to his own P.O. box numbers in several places.

DISBURSEMENTS

When making purchases the following procedures will assure good control:

1. Use prenumbered purchase orders as shown in Chapter 5.
2. When invoices come in for purchases, match them with the purchase orders.
3. Compare to see that you received merchandise and that prices are correct.
4. Re-add totals, discount computations, etc.
5. Make sure shipping charges are in line.
6. If at all possible, personally approve each bill for payment.
7. Always pay bills from invoices, not statements.
8. Mark invoices "paid" to avoid duplicate payment.

If an employee is authorized to sign checks, you should have a different employee authorize bills for payment, or do it yourself. You should also advise your bank of a limit for which employees may cash checks. If you set no limit, you may be liable for any amount, not only what you have in your account.

If you have a petty cash fund (see Chapter 4), you should make sure only one person has access to it, and personally approve each expenditure with your signature on a petty cash slip. If you want an employee to be authorized to do this, it should be a different employee from the one controlling the cash. You should avoid using petty cash funds for such things as paying temporary labor. In one company, whenever the employee in charge of petty cash needed extra cash, she made up a chit for a "day laborer" who did not exist and pocketed the cash. Her petty cash slips were not authorized individually, and were only reviewed when she needed to reimburse the petty cash fund. By then, her occasional phony slips were undetected among the many for "day laborers."

INVENTORY CONTROL

As discussed in Chapters 12 and 13, keeping a perpetual inventory will help you maintain control over it. When you take a physical inventory, compare it with the perpetual records. Differences could mean recording errors or theft.

Depending on the size and nature of your inventory, you may want a simple or elaborate system of control. Certainly, your company's stock should not be available to any employee without some form of control involving responsible authorization.

SUMMING UP

You may feel that the emphasis in this chapter has been on distrusting your employees. The facts are, however, that shoddy controls *encourage* employees to steal. There are times when personal financial pressures combined with clear-cut opportunity will change an ordinarily honest employee into a thief. Then there are those who *look* for ways to increase their "take home pay."

The honest employee will be grateful for a well-run, efficient system in which to work. There is no need for a suspicious attitude on your part if you have established a good internal control system. And since your life's savings may be at stake, make sure you do it.

18
Forms and Manual Systems

There are many forms and manual systems on the market which can help you accomplish your accounting procedures with speed and efficiency. Depending on the size of your business and the volume of recordkeeping, you may find one or more of the forms and systems described below applicable to your business.

BASIC TOOLS

You *could* handle all your recordkeeping with such simple tools as a piece of paper, a pencil, and your brain. Today most businesses, however, rely on other equipment such as adding machines, cash registers, and electronic calculators. The adding machine or calculator will save a lot of the time spent in adding, subtracting, etc. Cash registers are available in many models and prices, depending on what they can do. There are sophisticated electronic registers available today that can be tied directly into a computer for inventory control and other functions.

Basic paper forms for recordkeeping include analysis pads, columnar sheets, ledger sheets, post binders, ledger outfits, columnar books, account books, payroll and time records, order books, and receipt books. Other business forms you may use are invoices, purchase orders, statements, sales forms, etc.

These supplies can be purchased at your local stationers. If you can't find what you want there, or prefer to order by mail, write to the following companies for catalogs:

Better Records
National Blank Book Co., Inc
Holyoke, Mass. 01040
413-539-9811

Mattick Business Forms, Inc.
333 W. Hintz Rd., Box P
Wheeling, Il. 60090
312-541-7345

Rapidforms, Inc.
501 Beningo Blvd.
Bellmawr, N.J. 08031
800-257-8354

The Drawing Board, Inc.
P.O. Box 220505
Dallas, Texas 75222
800-527-9530

Watts Business Forms, Inc.
Division of Lewis Bus. Forms, Inc.
Dillsburg, Pa. 17019

New England Business Service, Inc.
Townsend, Mass. 01469
617-597-8715

Xerox Corporation
Route 303 & Bradley Rd.
Blauvelt, N.Y. 10913

SIMPLIFIED ACCOUNTING SYSTEMS

There are prepared forms and systems on the market that are set up to simplify your recordkeeping procedures by providing an organized system of recording and eliminating some of the writing steps.

Data Management, Inc., of Farmington, Connecticut, offers complete sets of looseleaf systems and supplies for bookkeeping. Figures 18.1, 18.2, and 18.3 illustrate three of the many forms available from Data Management, Inc.: (1) an annual payroll summary, (2) a capital and loan payment control sheet, and (3) an equipment cost worksheet. (Write to Data Management, Inc., for complete information on their looseleaf systems and supplies.)

There are several systems on the market that are designed to eliminate some of the writing steps in recordkeeping. For example, as you write a

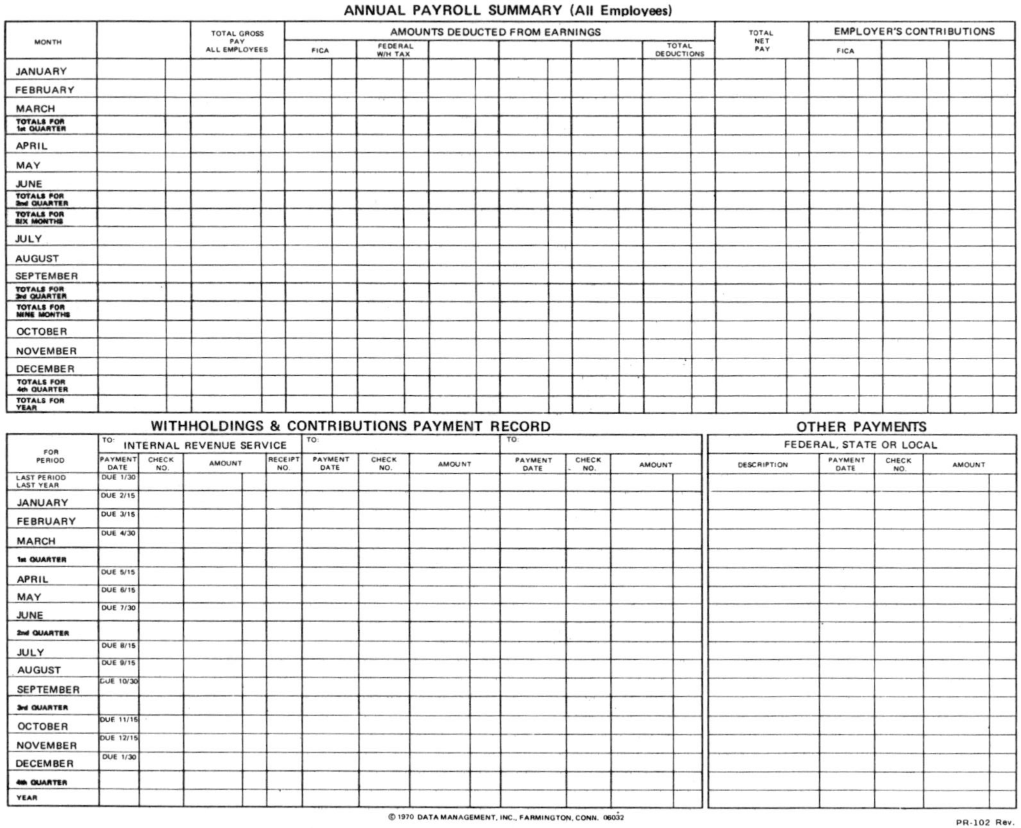

ANNUAL PAYROLL SUMMARY (All Employees)

MONTH		TOTAL GROSS PAY ALL EMPLOYEES	AMOUNTS DEDUCTED FROM EARNINGS					TOTAL NET PAY	EMPLOYER'S CONTRIBUTIONS		
			FICA	FEDERAL W/H TAX			TOTAL DEDUCTIONS		FICA		
JANUARY											
FEBRUARY											
MARCH											
TOTALS FOR 1st QUARTER											
APRIL											
MAY											
JUNE											
TOTALS FOR 2nd QUARTER											
TOTALS FOR SIX MONTHS											
JULY											
AUGUST											
SEPTEMBER											
TOTALS FOR 3rd QUARTER											
TOTALS FOR NINE MONTHS											
OCTOBER											
NOVEMBER											
DECEMBER											
TOTALS FOR 4th QUARTER											
TOTALS FOR YEAR											

WITHHOLDINGS & CONTRIBUTIONS PAYMENT RECORD

FOR PERIOD	TO: INTERNAL REVENUE SERVICE				TO:			TO:		
	PAYMENT DATE	CHECK NO.	AMOUNT	RECEIPT NO.	PAYMENT DATE	CHECK NO.	AMOUNT	PAYMENT DATE	CHECK NO.	AMOUNT
LAST PERIOD LAST YEAR	DUE 1/30									
JANUARY	DUE 2/15									
FEBRUARY	DUE 3/15									
MARCH	DUE 4/30									
1st QUARTER										
APRIL	DUE 5/15									
MAY	DUE 6/15									
JUNE	DUE 7/30									
2nd QUARTER										
JULY	DUE 8/15									
AUGUST	DUE 9/15									
SEPTEMBER	DUE 10/30									
3rd QUARTER										
OCTOBER	DUE 11/15									
NOVEMBER	DUE 12/15									
DECEMBER	DUE 1/30									
4th QUARTER										
YEAR										

OTHER PAYMENTS

FEDERAL, STATE OR LOCAL			
DESCRIPTION	PAYMENT DATE	CHECK NO.	AMOUNT

PR-102 Rev.

FIGURE 18.1. Annual Payroll Summary Form, available from Data Management, Inc., of Farmington, Connecticut.

CAPITAL AND LOAN PAYMENTS CONTROL 19____

DETAILED BREAKDOWN OF PAYMENTS ON LOANS AND CAPITAL ITEMS

HOLDER OF NOTE												
IDENTIFICATION												
ACTUAL FUNDS RECEIVED OR BALANCE TO BE FINANCED												
TOTAL FINANCE CHARGE												
TOTAL AMOUNT TO BE REPAID												
DATE 1st PAYMENT												
PAYMENT DUE DATE												
PAYMENT AMOUNT												
NUMBER OF PAYMENTS												
BAL. DUE START OF YR.												TOTALS
PAYMENTS JANUARY												
FEBRUARY												
MARCH												
APRIL												
MAY												
JUNE												
JULY												
AUGUST												
SEPTEMBER												
OCTOBER												
NOVEMBER												
DECEMBER												
TOTAL PAYMENTS THIS YEAR												
BAL. DUE END OF YEAR												

INTEREST												

FORM G 604

FIGURE 18.2. Capital and Loan Payment Control Sheet, available from Data Management, Inc., of Farmington, Connecticut.

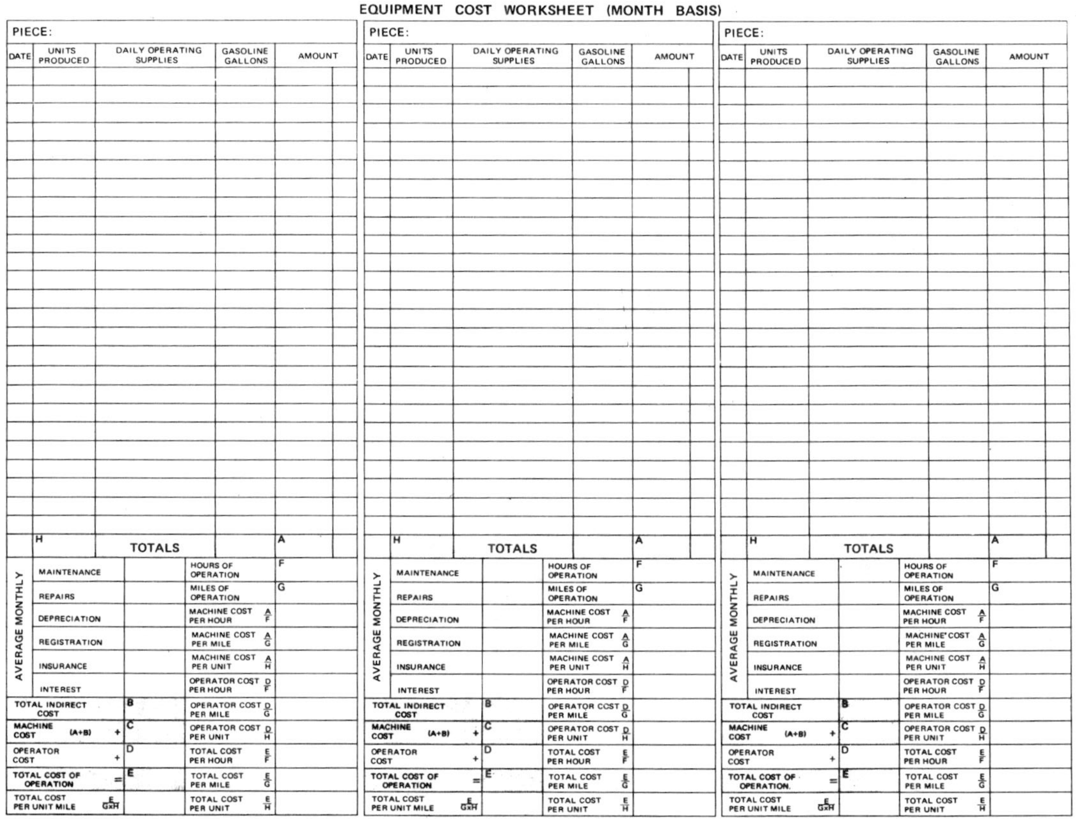

EQUIPMENT COST WORKSHEET (MONTH BASIS)

PIECE:

DATE	UNITS PRODUCED	DAILY OPERATING SUPPLIES	GASOLINE GALLONS	AMOUNT
	H	TOTALS		A

AVERAGE MONTHLY			
MAINTENANCE		HOURS OF OPERATION	F
REPAIRS		MILES OF OPERATION	G
DEPRECIATION		MACHINE COST PER HOUR $\frac{A}{F}$	
REGISTRATION		MACHINE COST PER MILE $\frac{A}{G}$	
INSURANCE		MACHINE COST PER UNIT $\frac{A}{H}$	
INTEREST		OPERATOR COST PER HOUR $\frac{D}{F}$	
TOTAL INDIRECT COST	B	OPERATOR COST PER MILE $\frac{D}{G}$	
MACHINE COST (A+B) +	C	OPERATOR COST PER UNIT $\frac{D}{H}$	
OPERATOR COST +	D	TOTAL COST PER HOUR $\frac{E}{F}$	
TOTAL COST OF OPERATION =	E	TOTAL COST PER MILE $\frac{E}{G}$	
TOTAL COST PER UNIT MILE $\frac{E}{G \times H}$		TOTAL COST PER UNIT $\frac{E}{H}$	

DATA MANAGEMENT, INC., FARMINGTON, CONN. 06032

FORM LG-2

FIGURE 18.3. Equipment Cost Worksheet, available from Data Management, Inc., of Farmington, Connecticut.

payroll check and stub, the information will be transferred through carbon backings to both an individual and total payroll summary. There are disbursement systems in which the check, check stub, remittance advice, disbursements journal, account distribution, and mailing envelope are all produced in one operation, and proved in one operation. There are similar systems for billing and receipts.

Figure 18.4 shows Shaw-Walker's payroll plan for firms that have five to 40 employees. Figure 18.5 shows their checkbook disbursements plan. For more information, call

Shaw-Walker Company
800-845-8350
201-248-4333

Other simplified accounting systems include: *Write It Once* from Burroughs Corp.; Peg-Rite from Master-Craft Corp.; and Safeguard Business Systems. They all use the same principle of writing an entry once which goes through carboned forms to various other records. For information on these systems, write to

Safeguard Business Systems
Lansdale, Pa., Los Angeles, Chicago, Atlanta
800-523-6660

Master-Craft Corp.
831 Cobb Ave.
Kalamazoo, Mich. 49007
616-345-2131

450 James P. Rodgers Dr.
Valdosta, Ga. 31601
912-244-7951

12804 South Spring St.
Los Angeles, Ca. 90061
213-749-7300

Burroughs Corp.
Business Forms and Supplies Group
1150 University Ave.
Rochester, New York
800-322-8178

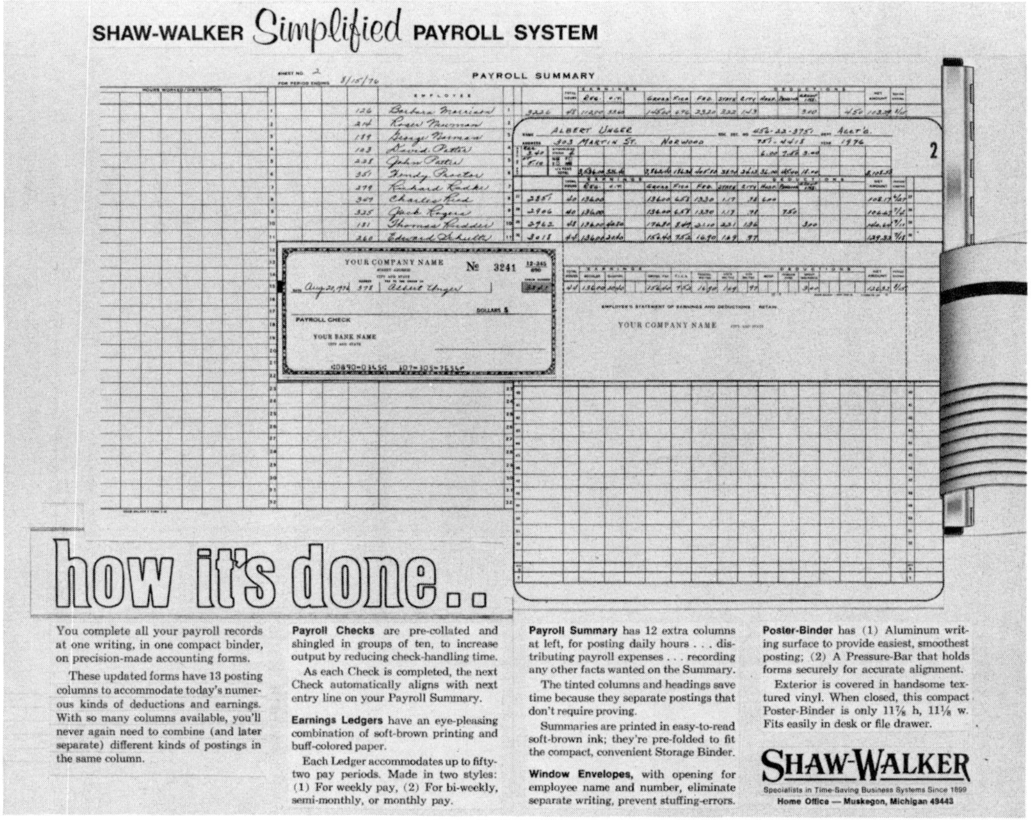

FIGURE 18.4. Payroll plan designed by Shaw-Walker Company to eliminate writing steps in record-keeping.

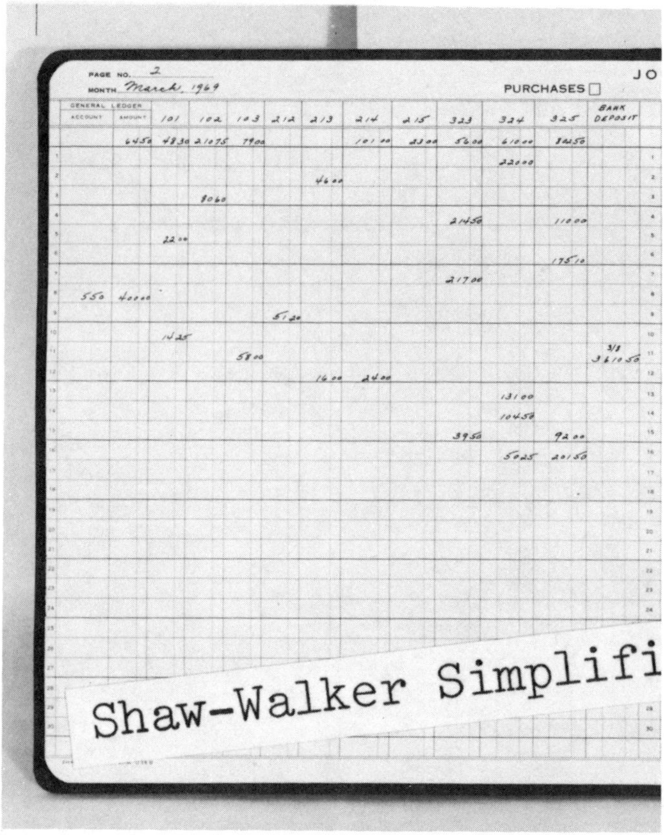

FIGURE 18.5. Checkbook Disbursements Plan designed by Shaw-Walker Company to eliminate writing steps in recordkeeping.

You may be able to find local offices for the above companies in your phone book.

INVENTORY CONTROL SYSTEMS

E-Z Way Systems manufactures inventory control systems ranging from 500 card to 18,000 card capacities (see sample cards in Figure 18.6). Their systems are effective in manually operated systems for inventory, production, tool room, maintenance, etc. For more information, write to

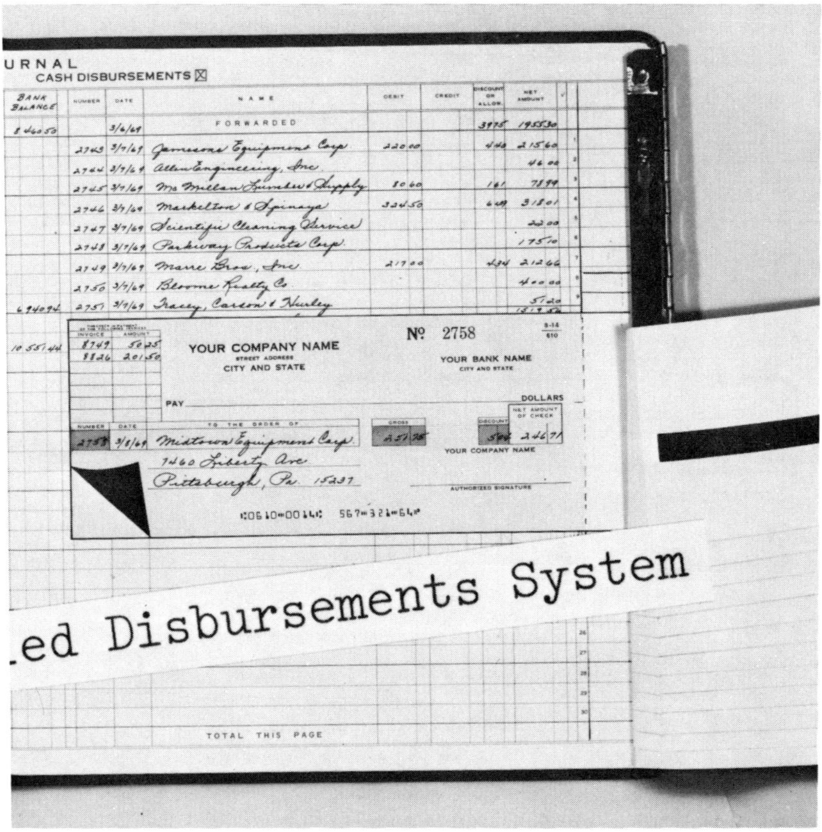

FIGURE 18.5. (Continued.)

E-Z Way Systems
Div. Industrial Automative, Inc.
Box No. 700
Newark, Ohio 43055

SUMMING UP

Once you understand the principles and procedures of accounting, you'll want to set up the simplest, most efficient system you can. You should take advantage of the forms and systems on the market to save recordkeeping

PART NUMBER	DESCRIPTION	STOCK LOCATION

SOURCE	SOURCE PART NO.	PRICING PER ______

REPLACES	STD. PKG.	WEIGHT PER ______	SHIP VIA	ECONOMICAL ORDER	REORDER POINT	REORDER QTY.

REPLACED BY	1	2	3	4	5	6	7	8	9	10	11	12	YEAR	TOTAL

PURCHASES				DISBURSEMENTS														
DATE	P.O. NO.	ORDER	RECD.	DATE	REFERENCE	IN	OUT	BAL.	DATE	REFERENCE	IN	OUT	BAL.	DATE	REFERENCE	IN	OUT	BAL.

TO BE ORDERED FORM 2-4 PART NO. © E-Z-WAY SYSTEMS NEWARK, OH. 43055 LITHO IN U.S.A. TO BE ORDERED

BACKORDER CARD

QUANTITY ______ PART NUMBER ______ MFG. ______

CUSTOMER OR USAGE ______

DATE ______ PUR. ORDER OR REQUISITION NUMBER ______

REMARKS ______

FILE THIS BACKORDER CARD PRECEDING THE CORRESPONDING INVENTORY CONTROL CARD

IF THIS NUMBER IS NOT A STOCK ITEM, FILE THIS CARD NUMERICALLY WITH INVENTORY CONTROL CARDS

OUR ORDER NUMBER ______ DATE ______

ORDERED FROM ______

REMARKS ______

ON ORDER FORM 3-1 PART NO. ON ORDER

FIGURE 18.6. Sample inventory cards are to be used with E-Z Way Systems inventory control systems.

costs, improve accuracy, and provide the necessary feedback for management decisions.

Even if your business is very small, there are manual forms and systems that are inexpensive and will improve the organization and efficiency of your accounting records. Whether or not a computerized accounting system will pay for itself in your company depends on the amount of processing you do and the volume of your business. See Chapter 19 for information on business computers.

19

Computerizing Your Business

Thomas E. Mitchell

Ten years ago, business computers were affordable by only the large corporations. Since then, advances in technology such as chip circuitry, silicon semiconductors, and laser photo engraving, have reduced the cost of manufacturing system components. This has resulted in an increase in the number of computer manufacturers, and a decrease in the cost of computing power.

Concurrent with the hardware advances have been software improvements. Software refers to the instructions (programs) which tell the computer what to do with the information (data) that you enter into the computer. Standard software packages are now available for even the smallest computers for most business recordkeeping functions.

These changes in the data processing field mean that you might want to change some of your manual procedures over to a computerized system. But buying a computer is not something you should do without careful planning. You'll need to invest time to learn enough about data processing to be able to make the right decisions.* Then you or someone else in your organization will need to spend a substantial amount of time implementing the new system.

In this chapter we'll discuss basic information about computers and how you might use them in your business. We'll also address many of the pitfalls you should avoid in your attempt to acquire data processing capabilities.

---

* The amount of material we can cover in this single chapter is limited. For more complete information, we recommend *Computer Basics,* a series of 36 weekly reports on the basics of data processing, published by INFORMATION PLUS, 175 Washington Valley Road, Warren, NJ 07060, Telephone 800–526–0794.

WHEN SHOULD YOU CONSIDER GETTING A COMPUTER?

As with any business effort, your objective in getting a computer must be to increase the net resources (profits) of your business—either through additional revenue generation or through cost reduction.

Computerization can provide this benefit in several ways:

Improved Operational Control. You make decisions and take actions based on information. For example, by looking at an aged accounts receivable report, you can see which accounts have past-due bills which require immediate action.

The computer can help you get information faster and more easily than you can with a manual system. Thus, you'll have more timely information to base your decisions on.

Labor Cost Savings. Processing information costs money, whether it's done manually or by a computer. But if you can eliminate the salary of a clerk by installing a computer, you may end up with a net savings.

Don't expect the savings to come instantly, though. Normally it takes *more* labor to get a computer system set up and operating on a day-to-day basis. Once it's running smoothly, however, much of the manual labor should be eliminated.

For example, it will take a clerk 100 times as long to type 100 invoices as to type one invoice. But once you have a computer program set up to print invoices, it's only a matter of running it a little longer to do more invoices.

Additional Management Information. A computer can do an enormous amount of analysis and print reports in numerous ways. Many of these analyses are almost impossible to produce manually.

For example, if you print invoices on a computer, you can save the information describing the items sold and print many reports about your company's sales. Such reports might include:

- Sales by geographic region
- Sales by class of merchandise
- Sales by season
- Sales by customer
- Sales by gross margin percentage

Report classifications can be combined so that you can print sales by gross margin within geographic area to identify where most of your margin dollars come from.

This type of analysis provides you with a better understanding of your business and can be the basis for profitable changes in your marketing, production, and pricing activities.

These, then, are the primary benefits you might expect to obtain from installing a computer in your business. There are also some common signs that usually indicate a computer might be helpful. For example:

- You require excessive clerical overtime
- You are unable to respond to customer inquiries in a timely fashion
- You are frustrated by an inability to deal with bookkeeping details
- You are afraid of losing key clerical personnel because your business would fall apart without them
- You don't have the current and thorough information you need to make decisions

As important as identifying the rationale for computerization is trying to estimate the *amount* of the benefit you think you can obtain in increased revenues or reduced costs. This isn't easy, but you *must* understand the possible magnitude of the benefit in order to decide whether or not to go ahead.

Be forewarned: if you don't know the dollars and cents benefits you can reasonably achieve *before* you acquire a computer, you're assuming an unnecessary risk!

WHAT SHOULD THE COMPUTER DO?

The application areas that are generally most beneficial to a small business are those that require a great deal of paper handling and for which an improvement in management control can produce worthwhile financial benefits. The following list presents the "best bets" for worthwhile computerization in your company:*

Decreasing Benefit To Your Company ↓	
	Billing and Accounts Receivable
	Inventory
	Sales Order Entry
	Accounts Payable
	Purchasing
	General Ledger
	Payroll

*The priorities here may shift, depending on the type of business you have. In a mail order business, for example, maintaining customer names and addresses and printing labels may be the number 1 "best bet" for a computer application.

(This list assumes that your company has capital tied up in the extension of credit to customers, and that you must maintain an inventory.)

Computerization of billing and accounts receivable generally provides the greatest benefit to a company. A great deal of clerical costs can usually be reduced, and analysis of sales information can provide many opportunities for additional revenues.

Payroll is usually the last priority because it doesn't tie up company resources. If your business is very labor intensive, however, and controlling labor costs is a factor in your success, a computerized payroll application may be the most rewarding choice.

WHAT IS DATA PROCESSING?

Data is information. *Processing* is the act of performing some procedure on (manipulating) that information, either manually or by machine. But today the term "data processing" refers strictly to the use of computers to manipulate information.

A data processing application can be divided into three major activities: input tasks, processing tasks, and output tasks.

Input tasks involve converting forms and documents *we* can read into *machine readable* media. This is usually accomplished by keying the information on a typewriter-like terminal, which transfers the keyed characters into punched holes on a card, or magnetic spots on disk or tape.

Processing tasks involve manipulating the input data in some way. This includes operations such as adding, subtracting, sorting, and comparing.

Output tasks produce the end product after input and processing. Output can be in human-readable or machine-readable form. Printing a report and displaying information on a CRT screen (Cathode Ray Tube terminal) are output activities which deliver information in human-readable form.

DATA PROCESSING OPTIONS

You can computerize part of your business without actually buying or leasing a computer. For example, you might use an outside service bureau to do the processing for you.

Your three main options for computerizing your business are:

- batch service bureaus
- remote job entry (time sharing)
- on site data processing

Batch service bureaus are companies that perform all your data processing functions at *their* location. You give them a "batch" of transactions and they perform all three data proccessing activities: input tasks, processing tasks, and output tasks.

For example, you might deliver a stack of invoices to the service bureau. They would enter the information from the invoices, process it, and return to you an invoice register, a sales analysis report, an accounts receivable trial balance, and statements to send to your customers.

Remote job entry (time sharing) provides another alternative. With this approach, you would perform the input tasks (and possibly the output tasks) at *your* location, with the processing tasks being done at the "remote" service bureau.

Normally you would have a terminal at your location to be used for entering data. This input would then be transferred via communications channels* to the computer at the service bureau. After the data was processed by the computer, it would be transmitted to your printer for output tasks. Or, the service bureau might print the output on their computer and deliver the end product to your company.

On site data processing, as the name implies, means that all three activities are performed by your company on a computer that you rent, lease, or own. Due to the dramatic drop in the costs of computer equipment, and the increase in computer processing power, on-site data processing has grown and will continue to grow at a substantial rate.

There are many variations on the above options for computerizing your business. The important thing is to understand the three elements of the processing cycle and how they are accomplished by any given method you may be considering (see Figure 19.1).

Recently the use of on site data processing has grown dramatically. Equipment and software costs have fallen into a range affordable by most companies. Another change is that now the operation of small business computers can be handled by non-technical employees. In addition, the hardware and software have become more reliable.

The result of all these changes is an explosion in the small business computer market. An associated trend is a downturn in the use of service bureaus.

Because of the phenomenal growth in the small business computer market, the affordability of this method of automation, and the advantages

---

* means of transmitting data over telephone lines, cable, or microwave

	Data Processing Tasks		
	Input	Processing	Output
Batch Service Bureau	Outside	Outside	Outside
Remote Job Entry (Time Sharing)	Company	Outside	Company
On Site	Company	Company	Company

FIGURE 19.1. Basic data processing approaches.

of on-site computing, we'll limit the rest of this chapter to a discussion of these machines:

- what they are
- how they might be used
- their approximate cost
- how to go about installing one

SMALL BUSINESS COMPUTERS: WHAT ARE THEY?

Basically there are two kinds of business computers that a small company would consider acquiring. They are the personal computer (sometimes called a microcomputer) and the minicomputer. An example of a personal computer is the Radio Shack TRS 80, and an example of the minicomputer is the IBM System/34.

There are many differences between these two categories, and a difference that is immediately obvious is the cost. As we publish, a personal computer can range anywhere from $150 up to about $10,000. The minicomputer can cost anywhere from $10,000 up to about $150,000.

The second difference is again obvious—the physical size of the computer itself. A personal computer can range from a hand-held extended capability calculator to a table top unit which can include a CRT (Cathode Ray Tube) terminal (with keyboard), a diskette unit, and a central processing unit (CPU). A minicomputer, on the other hand, generally starts about the size of a small desk (but contains basically the same components as the personal computer). A large minicomputer might require the space of a small business office and have, in some cases, in excess of ten CRT terminals attached to it.

The minicomputer is larger and more expensive because of its expanded capabilities. A mini has more *main* (internal storage) memory space than a personal computer. It can hold more data and programs without as much swapping between *main* memory and external storage (disk or tape). This means the minicomputer can process a great deal more information in a shorter period of time. Most personal computers are limited in the number of transactions they can store and process.

For example, many of the personal computers have accounts receivable packages. But the maximum number of customers that can be processed by these programs is 500. On the minicomputer, however, that limitation might be as high as 50,000 customers. Quite a difference.

Another difference is that a personal computer is usually a single user system; that is, only one operator can utilize the system at a time. Whereas several operators (in fact, for some machines, upwards of 20) may use a minicomputer.

The last major difference is the speed at which the computer operates. A minicomputer may operate as much as 6 to 7 times faster than a personal computer in terms of how quickly it can read (input), process, and print (output) information.

Despite the differences discussed above, personal computers and minicomputers operate in the same manner. They accept input information, process that information, and produce output reports and files.

The chart in Figure 19.2 shows the major differences between personal (microcomputers), minicomputers, and mainframe (very large) computers.

SMALL BUSINESS COMPUTERS: HOW CAN YOU USE ONE?

Earlier we outlined various areas of business for which computer processing could be advantageous. Now let's take one of those areas and examine, step by step, how that processing would typically occur. Our example will be an accounts receivable application.

The objectives of the accounts receivable system (both computerized and manual) are (1) to control the accuracy of the amounts of money due you as a result of the sale of a product or performance of a service, and (2) to promote the ease of collecting those dollars owed to you. Consistent with our prior discussion, an accounts receivable system requires three basic elements: the input of data, the processing of that data, and the production of reports and files.

In order to maintain a computerized accounts receivable system, your first step must be to establish a customer master file. This is a computer file that contains the customer's name, address, phone number, and the total amount

GENERALLY . . .	PERSONAL (MICRO COMPUTER)	MINICOMPUTER	MAINFRAME
EXAMPLE	Apple II Plus	Basic 4	IBM 370
USE	Personal and Small Business	Small to Medium Business	Large Business
HARDWARE COST	$500 to $10,000	$10,000 to $150,000	$150,000 Plus
SOFTWARE COST (per application)	Hundreds	Thousands	Varies
STORAGE*	32–64 K (0 to 10 Megabytes)	32–512 K (10–125 Megabytes)	512K Plus
PERSONNEL TO OPERATE	Some Training	More Extensive Training	Computer Professionals

*Storage refers to the amount of information the computer can hold at one time. A byte is one character (the letter A, for example). 1 K = 1,024 bytes. 1 Megabyte = one million bytes.

FIGURE 19.2.

of dollars owed to your company. Before any other transactions can be processed for this customer, the customer master file must be available.

In order to reduce data storage requirements, all customers will be assigned a number—a customer number. This number will then be used to identify each transaction related to that particular customer. Using a customer number eliminates the need to store the customer name for each transaction.

Once you have established a customer master file record, you can "process transactions." These transactions include the entry of sales invoices, checks or cash received, and adjustments made to a customer's account to correct an error or write off an uncollectible balance. These transactions will be entered and written onto an accounts receivable transaction file (inside the computer) and will usually be printed by transaction type. The resulting reports will include the sales register (a listing of the invoices entered), the cash receipts, and the adjustments to the customers' accounts (normally done through a general journal in a manual system). The primary processing that will occur in the accounts receivable system is the addition of monthly transactions to the customer master file. This is akin to the posting process in a manual system.

For accounts receivable there are basically two kinds of processing that may occur: a system may be a balance-forward system or an open-item system. In a balance-forward system, just the balance at the end of the month (after transactions are processed) remains on the customer's account. In an open-item system, the details of all unpaid invoices and unapplied cash receipts are retained in the accounts receivable master file.

One result of your accounts receivable processing will be a new accounts receivable master file, which you will use to start off the following month. Another result is usually a series of reports including the accounts receivable trial balance, aging report, cash receipts list, invoice list/sales register, and adjustments journal.

One of the advantages of data processing is the ability to sort, evaluate, and print information that already exists in a file—a process that might require a prohibitive amount of time in a manual system. In your accounts receivable system you could determine the average amount of time it takes you to collect monies from each customer, the amount of sales you make to each customer, sales by geographical area based on the customer's zip code, and many other facts that may have value in the operation of your company.

SMALL BUSINESS COMPUTERS: APPLICATION PACKAGES

The basic functions of accounting are nearly identical from one company to the next, with exceptions occurring due to the nature of the company's business. This fact has allowed computer manufacturers and independent software vendors to develop standard application programs for these accounting areas. Without exception, you'll be able to find an accounts receivable software package for a particular computer.

The presence of such application packages provides you with computer capability at a lower cost and a lower risk than having the system designed and programmed specifically for your needs. Generally these applications have been thoroughly tested by other users, come with complete documentation and operating instructions, and contain most of the features you would like to have for your business. The cost of the software is much lower because the development and programming expenses are spread over a large number of users.

There can be problems, however, with a packaged program. You should never simply take a salesperson's word that a particular software package will be right for your company. You may require modifications made to the packaged program, and this could cost a substantial amount. You may find that you outgrow a package, for example, and there is no provision in it for expansion. As you'll see below, software as well as hardware purchases should be made with care. One way to check out a software package *before* you buy it is to purchase the manual first. This small investment will enable you to get a better idea whether the actual program will fit your needs.

HOW TO ACQUIRE A SMALL BUSINESS COMPUTER

The purchase of a computer system must be approached with great care. The watch words in selecting data processing equipment are "buyer beware."

As mentioned earlier, a computer system is a large investment in time and money, and golf courses are covered with echoes of war stories about those investments turning into nightmares. There is such a variety of equipment, software, and services available, that making an intelligent decision is difficult. You can't expect much help from vendor salespeople, either, because they'll try to make your need fit their product even if their product doesn't fit your need. Remember, they are trying to make a sale, and they often do not *know* enough about your business (or their computers) to make an accurate analysis of their system's usefulness to you.

First and foremost, we recommend you get sound advice—from your accountant or a consultant who is not tied to a particular manufacturer or software vendor. Before seeking another's judgment, however, make sure that they have good judgment in the area of computers. Find out first if a particular consultant has helped others (in similar businesses) to acquire computers, and how they fared from the advice.

Another approach is for you yourself to learn enough about data processing, and the hardware and software on the market, to make a purchase decision. If you decide to go this route, here are some suggestions:

- Make a list of all the functions you want your system to handle. Be specific, and include estimates of growth over the next 3 years.
- Be conservative. Look at equipment which has been around for a while, from vendors who have been in business long enough, and are large enough, to back up their machines and software.
- Make sure maintenance service will be available *on your premises,* and within 24 hours. Find out about back-up provisions in case the equipment is down longer than 24 hours and you must get work out.
- Ask to talk to technicians and service engineers as well as salespeople. Ask the toughest questions you can think of, and ask them to explain anything you don't understand in *plain terms,* not computer jargon.
- When you've narrowed down your choice, ask for the names of other similar businesses which have installed that particular equipment. Talk to those people and find out how they're doing. Try to go and see the equipment in operation, producing the kind of work you will be doing.

- Get a detailed proposal from the vendor, in writing, which spells out exactly what equipment, software, and technical support will be supplied. If they promise any particular capabilities for your business, have these put in writing also.
- If your're buying a microcomputer, you'll find that most of them have similar capabilities. The big differences lie in the software, and this is the area you should concentrate on first.

SMALL BUSINESS COMPUTERS: BUY vs. LEASE

In making your buy or lease decision, the single most important consideration is the length of time the system is likely to be able to handle your data processing requirements. Will there be room for system expansion—both with regard to the processor and the peripheral equipment (printer, terminals, etc.)? In most cases, it's not wise to make your first system the most powerful one offered by a particular vendor. If your company's operations expand, how will you expand the system?

Generally, if you're confident that a particular system can handle your data processing needs for *three to five years,* then purchasing will be advantageous. But if you've selected a top of the line model, or there are fewer than three years of potential use in the system, you're probably better off to lease.

One word of caution: take a close look at any leasing agreement you may be considering. We've found that the effective rate of interest on leasing agreements over the last several years has run close to ten percent *over* the prime rate. If you have alternate sources of financing, you should consider them.

SUMMING UP

Just about any small business today must *consider* getting a computer. Very often a single function, placed on the computer, will cover the total costs of equipment, software, and maintenance.

Computers *can* be invaluable to a small business. But they can also be deadly. To be safe, learn all you can. Take one step at a time. And go with reputable vendors.

Index